D0742202

HOW YOU CAN PROFIT

FROM THE COMING DEVALUATION

$ $ $ $ $

HARRY BROWNE

$ $ $ $ $

HOW YOU
CAN PROFIT
FROM THE COMING
DEVALUATION

$ $ $ $ $

PROPERTY OF
CLACKAMAS COMMUNITY COLLEGE
LIBRARY

ARLINGTON HOUSE   *New Rochelle, N.Y.*

HG
4921
.B76

THIRD PRINT[█████████████████████████]

Copyright © 1970 by Arlington House, New Rochelle, New York.
All rights reserved. No portion of this book may be reproduced without written permission from the publisher, except by a reviewer who may quote brief passages in connection with a review.

Library of Congress Catalog Card Number 77-101959

SBN 87000—073—X

MANUFACTURED IN THE UNITED STATES OF AMERICA

TO JOAN

43258

Gift (William F. Berda)

Acknowledgments

In the text of this book, I've attempted to call attention to the sources of various ideas cited. Wherever possible, I have mentioned the names of the individuals who are responsible for passing the ideas on to me.

In addition, however, I'm very grateful to several individuals for more general aid in helping me to comprehend this subject. In the field of money, the most important help has come from the writings of Murray Rothbard. Also, I appreciate the explanations of Henry Hazlitt and Wilmot Hunter.

With regard to the development of precise explanations and definitions, I've learned a great deal from Alvin Lowi and Andrew Galambos.

Also, I'm grateful to senior editor Llewellyn Rockwell for polishing off the rough edges in the text. And to Arlington House for its willingness to publish books with uncommon viewpoints.

Needless to say, I am the only person responsible for any conclusions reached in this book.

Table of Contents

HOW YOU CAN PROFIT

FROM THE COMING DEVALUATION

$ $ $ $ $

$ CHAPTER 1 $

The New Millionaires

$ $ $ $ $

BETWEEN 1929 AND 1939, MILLIONS OF AMERICANS LOST BILLIONS of dollars in savings and investments. The stories have been told and retold so many times that we tire of hearing them.

But forgotten are the thousands of Americans who made their fortunes during the same period of time. These are the people who "sold short" during 1929. They are the ones who removed their cash from banks *before* they closed, and then used their cash to buy businesses and homes when prices were at rock bottom and no one else had any cash.

It's not that they preyed on the misfortunes of others. Rather, they had the foresight to see what was coming and to provide for themselves accordingly. They made big profits and their new wealth formed the foundation of the new economy. They were the ones who could produce and hire and provide when others were in need. They became the new heroes of the economy, just by believing in themselves and looking out for themselves.

Some people say that such days will never return to America— that depressions and crises have been legislated out of existence. Others say that economic cycles are a way of life in any nation that uses inflation to finance the growth of government.

Perhaps the best way to get at the truth is to review the state of the nation briefly, to see what might be coming.

A look at the nation's financial strength indicates a prosperous America. There are more people working than ever before. Stock market prices, while constantly fluctuating, are in their all-time high range.

Steel production is at 90% of capacity. Other basic American industries are setting new production records. There are more products and services available.

Underlying this news is an overwhelming sense of confidence. Our last President described the nation's economic condition as being "absolutely sound." And the man in the White House today has declared the time is in sight when "poverty will be banished from the nation."

Many famous experts believe the nation is now "depression-proof"—with many reasons to support this view.

For example, the Federal Reserve System has a host of powers with which to expand the money supply and to keep the economy balanced and moving upward. A steady flow of credit is available for business expansion, and to counteract any trends toward high interest rates or falling wages.

In addition, there is an intricate structure of governmental programs to undergird the economy: public works, highway construction, farm programs, anti-monopoly controls, taxing policies, stock market regulation, and a multitude of other federal powers.

The small amounts of gold leaving the federal Treasury are generally considered to be of little consequence. After all, it's widely agreed that our nation's currency is backed up by the great productive strength of the people, not by a yellow metal.

In view of all this, it's no wonder that the United States is considered depression-proof. It's no wonder that many people believe our government is capable of creating permanent prosperity.

What do *you* think?

Do these federal programs and powers give you the confidence to see an unbroken cycle of prosperity ahead? Do you feel that economic crises have been eliminated once and for all?

If you do, you'd better go back and reread those news items. You weren't reading about present-day America. *It was America of the 1920s.*

Every statement you've just read was taken from the news reports of 1928–1929—when America, through federal economic control, had supposedly become depression-proof—when Federal Reserve monetary controls and public works and farm programs and other federal powers had created what most people thought was an invincible prosperity—when President Hoover announced a "New Attack on Poverty," described as "business guided by measurements instead of hunches . . . economics for an age of science."

Yes, this was America of October 28, 1929—the day before panic hit the stock market and the Dow-Jones Industrial Averages dropped 12% in one day.

Yes, this was the America that preceded the economic collapse that caused businesses to fail all over the nation.

Yes, this was the America that caused bank runs which led to banks shutting their doors on their depositors and the loss of millions of dollars in savings accounts.

And ten years later, the unemployed in America still numbered over nine million.

"It couldn't happen here."

But it did.[1]

There is more to the story, however. For this was also the America that led to new fortunes—as farsighted individuals took their limited resources and invested them in ways that would go way up, instead of way down.

The purpose of this review of the twenties isn't to prove that depressions are inevitable. They aren't. They are the direct effect of certain economic causes. If the causes do not occur, the depressions will not occur.

But at the same time, when those causes *do* occur, the effects are inevitable.

Our review of the 1928–1929 news reports demonstrates one

1. An excellent economic history of America, 1921–1933, is Rothbard: *America's Great Depression*, listed in the bibliography.

thing. All the confidence in the world, all the powers that politicians can think of, and all the good intentions man can muster are not proper protection for your savings and investments. Nothing will ever replace your own knowledge and understanding as the proper safeguard for your future.

There's very little difference between the financial world of today and that of 45 years ago. At that time, the investor was told that the economy had become too complicated for the average person to understand. He was told there was little reason to worry, however, for the government now had the power to create a new age of permanent prosperity. All one had to do was to leave his fate in the hands of the "experts."

Many millions of Americans did just that. But the experts were wrong. And the millions of Americans lost their life savings.

But there were also those who didn't buy the prevailing myths. They had confidence in their own minds. They provided for themselves, regardless of what the crowds around them chose to do. And they didn't lose, they won.

There are a few of them around today, too. They see through the clichés and government-worship that blind so many. They trust their own minds and look to the future. They see something different from what they've been told. And they're preparing for it.

We're on the threshold of great changes. During the next five years or so, we'll most likely go through another economic revolution. It may be more far-reaching than the last one was.

For example, a devaluation of the dollar is almost inevitable. How will that affect *you?* Superficial commentaries in the newspapers indicate that you won't be affected at all. And yet the truth (as this book will prove) is that many individuals will make great profits from a devaluation—and others will suffer great losses.

You don't have to rely upon the superficial appraisals of the so-called experts. These matters aren't beyond your ability to understand. You can determine for yourself what is likely to happen, how it will affect you, and what you can do to profit from the situation.

In fact, that's what this book is all about. It's designed to show you how relatively simple the world of economics is. You'll see how one thing inevitably leads to another.

It's not a long book, because the subject isn't nearly so complicated as we're continually told it is.

It is not a book full of abstract formulas, because the matter is much more real and practical and personal than the manner in which it's usually described.

You *can* understand it. You can act upon the principles involved. And you can use the coming events as the springboard for your new fortune.

Or you can ignore the whole matter and suffer from that which you don't understand.

The choice is wholly yours.

THE ROLE OF MONEY

It all has to do with the simple little word *money*. Everything flows from the way the money system is handled. It is the cause of inflation, of depressions, of any sudden changes in the economy.

Not one person in a thousand really understands what money is. And yet, there are few subjects in the world more fascinating than the study of money. A proper grasp of it will give you the key that unlocks the many puzzles of national economic events.

In the first 70 pages of this book, we can cover 99% of all you need to know about *money* and its effect upon the economy. Then we'll proceed to develop a specific course of action that will enable you to profit from the events that are inevitably coming in the next few years.

$ CHAPTER 2 $

What Is Money?

$ $ $ $ $

WHERE DO WE BEGIN?

Let's go right back to the very basics, so there can be no misunderstanding between us as we proceed to the conclusions.

It you were to find yourself alone on an isolated island, you'd have no need for a medium of exchange. There would be no one with whom to exchange.

You would go to work, as necessary, to produce the things you needed for your survival. You'd produce some things that you would want to consume immediately, and you would probably produce other things to be stored for later consumption.

You might also produce some other things that would be called "capital goods"—things that make further production easier. But you would only produce when you believed it would lead ultimately to something you wanted.

Not hard to understand, is it?

Let's suppose now that there was one other person on the island with you. Each of you has his own area of the island and each of you is producing for himself.

Sooner or later, you'd probably begin exchanging things with each other. Perhaps you've produced more than you need of something he hasn't produced, and vice versa. You exchange your surplus with each other—and both of you profit thereby.

Obviously, you won't trade your production for something you have no use for. Why bother working if your efforts don't eventually bring you something you can use? You'll trade only for those things you want to use now or can store for use at a later date.

And here we have a very important rule at work, one that we should file mentally for reference later on: *You only produce and exchange when you believe it will lead ultimately to something you want.*

On such a simple basis, with only one or two people involved, it's very easy to see and understand what's happening. You're producing and exchanging in order to acquire the things you'll eventually use to further your own well-being.

But now let's suppose there are 100 people on the island— each with his own area. You will still have to produce to survive; there's no way to avoid that.

But exchanges will probably take place on a much wider basis. In fact, it will be only a matter of time until a "specialization of labor" develops. That's where an individual no longer produces everything for himself. Instead, he concentrates on the production of only one or two items—and then trades his production with others for the products and services he wants.

You know that no one's going to exchange with you if you don't have something he wants. So you'll gear your production to those things that are in demand by others. In that way, you'll get the most possible in return.

These trades with others are called *direct exchange*—the trading of some of your property for another commodity you intend to use yourself. This is also called *barter*—trading without money.

The direct exchanges are a natural step in the development of a civilized society.

INDIRECT EXCHANGE

But, eventually, you find yourself in a position where you're willing to accept in exchange an item you don't intend to use. You accept it only to improve your trading position with someone else.

Suppose you have butter and you're looking for wheat. I have wheat, but I'm *not* looking for butter. Instead, I need corn. So you go find a third person who has corn and is looking for butter. You trade your butter for his corn. Then you come back to me and trade the corn for my wheat.

You have what you want; but it took two exchanges to get it.

This is the beginning of *indirect exchange*—the trading of one thing for something you don't intend to use yourself.

For example, one day Jones the nail-maker walks into the store of Smith the furniture-maker (whose store is conveniently located under a palm tree). Jones opens the conversation with, "Smith, I need a new workbench. I'll give you 2,000 nails to make one for me."

"Sorry," says Smith, "I have all the nails I'll need for awhile. Those you gave me for the bed I made for you will last me for another six months. Come back and see me then."

Determined not to be refused, Jones goes on, "But I need the workbench *now!* Look, you're bound to use those nails eventually. But, even in the meantime, you can probably trade them to someone else for something you need. I'm always getting offers of trades from people wanting nails. They're a lot easier to exchange than furniture."

"You have a point there," ponders Smith. "I do seem to have a lot of trouble exchanging kingsize beds for clothes. This way, I'd use only as many nails as I need for each purchase . . . well, okay—I'll try anything once."

So he accepts the nails and makes the workbench for Jones. And then he goes out to find products for which he can exchange the nails.

And, lo and behold, it works! He finds that trades are much easier to make. As a result, he enjoys life a lot more with a few nails in his pocket. He can stop at a store and trade for anything he wants to—without having to arrange an elaborate, long-term furniture purchase with the storekeeper.

In fact, he merely points out to the merchant the advantages of nails as a trading medium in the same way that Jones pointed them out to him. And the final argument is that you can always use the nails *sometime* in the future; they won't lose their value. And if *you* don't use them, *someone* will.

The merchant realizes this; and so he accepts the nails, confident that he can use them or trade them for what he wants.

In the months to follow, Jones the nail-maker notices a slow, steady increase in the demand for his product. Why? Because individuals, *one at a time*, are coming to see that it's valuable to have a few extra nails on hand (in addition to those needed for construction purposes) to facilitate exchanges with others.

Nails seem to most people on the island to be an ideal trading medium. But once there are enough nails around for that purpose, the demand will level off. The nails are not free; they cost Jones his time to make them and he demands something in return when he trades them with others. So no one's going to pay for more nails than he'll find useful to have.

As a result, once there are enough nails in circulation to facilitate exchange, there'll be no additional value from more nails. In other words, like any other commodity, they seek their natural level of quantity, their market price.

Let's go back a moment to the point we recognized on page nine: *You only produce and exchange when you believe it will lead ultimately to something you want.*

Smith, the furniture-maker, didn't produce the workbench just for the sake of producing. In his eyes, his profit didn't come from the number of beds or workbenches produced.

Neither did his satisfaction come from the number he sold. To be able to say he sold a certain number of pieces of furniture was of no particular value to him.

To Smith, the object of it all was to obtain the things he wanted. He produced and sold furniture with only one purpose in mind—to trade it for the specific things *he* wanted. So he wouldn't make a workbench just to be making a workbench. Nor would he accept nails just so he could say he'd made a sale.

He agreed to Jones's offer only when he was convinced it was a step toward getting what he wanted.

And this is a vital point. Neither production volume nor sales volume is ever the object. It's only what you eventually receive for it that counts. You only produce and exchange when you believe it will lead ultimately to something you want.

We will have occasion to come back to this seemingly obvious point as we proceed. But, meanwhile, we see that this simple little trade has been the seed from which indirect exchange is born on the island.

And as it naturally grows in use and acceptance, it opens up all kinds of new possibilities for residents of the community. Now it's possible for one man to employ another, paying him with nails instead of with fractions of a house. Now long-term capital investments can be made—by trading one's production for nails, purchasing capital goods with the nails, making a new product, and finally selling it.

So nails have become money. And what is money?

Money is a commodity that is accepted in exchange by an individual who intends to trade it for something else.

Money is a commodity, just like anything else that's traded in the marketplace. What distinguishes a money commodity from other commodities is the intention of the recipient to keep it only until he trades it to someone else. It's only a means to a further exchange for that recipient.

Not *everyone* intends to trade it, however. Some people receive the money commodity, intending to use it for its own natural purpose (in this case, nails for construction purposes).

And this brings us to the key word in the definition of money: *accepted*. The commodity can become money only when an individual *accepts* it—when someone's willing to take it, confident that he can trade it ultimately for what *he* wants.

You only produce and exchange when you believe it'll lead

ultimately to something you want. So you won't accept bamboo reeds—just because someone wants something you have.

The commodity to be used as money must already have established itself as being in demand—otherwise, you'd never be sure that you could trade it later for something you wanted.

Because of this, the money commodity is never chosen by a majority vote; it's never initially imposed upon a community by the government; it's never collectively nor arbitrarily selected. It *evolves—one exchange at a time*—as one individual and then another decide to accept it in exchange.

Governments can only choose to go along with what's naturally evolved in the marketplace. If they stray from that, they're doomed to destruction. For money only takes on value as individuals are willing to accept it. But we'll come back to governments later.

To summarize, the money commodity will emerge, one exchange at a time, as each individual sees the commodity, evaluates it, and agrees to accept it—believing this will further his ability to obtain eventually the items he wants.

In our island example, the individual accepted the nails because he knew how much they were worth in terms of other commodities; and he knew that, come what may, they'd always be of some value to him. He knew he'd never be "stuck" with nails because he could also use them himself.

As we've seen, the volume of nails would be determined by the number of nails that proved useful in exchange, together with the normal demand for nails in construction. Beyond that, any additional production of nails by Jones would be worthless to him; more nails would simply lessen the exchange value of each nail. So he'd be working harder (producing more nails) but getting no more in return.

If he were to try to demand more for his nails than individuals were willing to give (the market value), he'd be inviting competition. For someone else could then offer nails at a lower exchange price; or possibly even offer a more useful commodity as a medium of exchange.

So Jones's success will still depend upon his technical ability and

marketing sense; he has no special advantage just because he's
the man who produces the money commodity.

WHY GOLD AND SILVER?

It's quite possible that more than one commodity might be
used as money—either in the same or in neighboring communities.
The only question that matters is: will an individual be willing
to accept the commodity in an exchange?

But it is only natural that consumers will begin to rely upon
the one or two commodities that best satisfy their needs and
desires in exchanges. Despite the hundreds of different commodities
that have been used as money at various times and places in
history, two commodities have dominated the money markets for
centuries. They are *gold* and *silver*.

But why gold and silver?

As we've seen, the development would have had to be purely
natural—one exchange at a time—adding up to billions of trades.
No one person or group ever decided that it would be so. But,
in retrospect, we can look back and understand *why* gold and silver
became supreme.

There are five main attributes of gold and silver that give
individuals good reason to *accept* these commodities confidently:

1. Both commodities are *durable*. They can be stored for long
periods of time, if necessary, without perishing. Obviously,
bananas won't do. Imagine saving up for a new car, then going
to the closet to take out your savings, only to find they had rotted.

2. The commodities are easily *divisible*. As we saw, it was easier
to exchange nails than furniture because you could divide a supply
of nails into small purchases. And gold and silver can be broken
into smaller pieces or used as dust—without harming their
inherent value in any way.

3. Gold and silver are relatively *convenient* to handle. Their
naturally high market values make it possible to work with small
quantities. Paper wouldn't do—because you'd need so much of
it to be worth a desired item that it would be inconvenient to
carry and exchange.

4. Gold and silver are each *consistent* in quality. Once it has been assayed and its fineness determined, one ounce of gold is as good as any other ounce of the same fineness. This simplifies exchange negotiations.

For short periods in history, each of these four rules has been violated by various commodities that still managed to serve adequately as money. But for a commodity to suffice as money, a fifth attribute is absolutely necessary. For we're talking about human beings whose futures and securities are at stake. And they won't produce and exchange unless they believe it will lead ultimately to something useful.

This means the individual must be confident that what he is receiving today will be exchangeable tomorrow. And how can he be sure of that?

5. The commodity must have *accepted value*. It must be usable and accepted for a non-money purpose before it can serve as money. Only then can the recipient be sure he isn't receiving a white elephant.

Gold is a commodity—just like lettuce, nails, bricks, or toothpaste. Gold has its own uses. In fact, gold and silver are used for such things as jewelry, dental work, electronics, art objects, ornamentation, soldering, photography, and other purposes. If gold weren't money, it would still circulate in the world because of its other uses. (We normally refer to the non-money uses as *commercial* or *industrial* uses.)

So you never have to worry about gold going out of style as a money item. Its continued value is based upon something sure and reliable. If your neighbor refuses to accept it in exchange from you, you can still take it to a jeweler or a dental supply company and receive something of value for it.

That previously determined value also tells you *how much* gold is worth in relationship to other commodities. If the money commodity didn't have that separate value, you couldn't confidently accept it in trade for what you have produced, for you wouldn't know the worth of what you received.

Gold, as either an industrial or monetary commodity, is subject to the same laws of supply and demand as is any other commodity: Overproduction will cause its market value to drop.

On the other hand, a *shortage* of gold would increase its value and thereby encourage prospecting and production. There has never really been a long-term shortage of gold in the world; and there certainly isn't one today. It is being produced at an ever increasing rate.

But we're getting ahead of ourselves. The evolution of our money system must continue.

Up to this point, we've recognized two important signposts that will have great significance when we get to the practical application of these principles of money:

1. You only produce and exchange when you believe it will lead ultimately to something you want.

2. Money is a commodity that is accepted in exchange by an individual who intends to trade it for something else.

Putting these two together, we find that you would not accept "money" in exchange if you didn't believe it would lead to the purchase of an item you really wanted.

That leads us to some further developments in money. In the next few pages, we'll see the transition from the primitive society— our island example, employed to isolate the purpose of each individual in an exchange—to the modern, complicated economy in which we live.

CHAPTER 3

What Is Paper?

$ $ $ $ $

IN ANY MARKET, THE NATURAL IMPULSE OF AN AMBITIOUS individual is to look around for ways of making life easier for other people—knowing they will pay him a handsome profit for what he makes available to them.

One enterprising fellow notices that individuals waste a lot of time measuring gold dust in exchange for their drinks at the bar.

So he opens a mint. He buys raw gold or silver from miners and converts the metal into coins. He stamps the coins with his name and the amount of gold inside the coin.

If an individual trusts the coin-maker, he will probably prefer to use the coin in exchange. Its recognizable weight makes it easier than measuring gold dust.

But since no one wants to trade for something that may be worthless, he must be sure there's really gold (in the amount indicated) inside the coin. Not only that, he has to know that *others* will accept the coin, too.

The coins must be stamped with the seal of someone who has gained widespread respect in the marketplace. For an individual will be willing to accept the coin only when he's sure of the value of the commodity in the coin.[1]

Exchange is made easier as individuals trade coins instead of continually measuring gold dust.

But the evolution continues. Another ambitious chap opens a warehouse. "Bring your gold to me," he says. "I'll store it for you in my theft-proof vault. I'll give you a receipt for your gold, so you can claim it any time you want it. I only charge a small fee for the service of storing it for you."

This means you can now keep your gold in a safe warehouse—rather than having it at home where it could be stolen.

You have the receipts in your possession; you can take them to the warehouse and get your gold whenever you need it.

And as the use of the warehouse becomes more widespread, and the integrity of the warehouseman becomes known, the receipts can serve an additional purpose. You can exchange the receipts themselves.

Why bother going to the warehouse to get your gold, only to trade it to someone who will probably take it back to the same warehouse for safekeeping? Instead, you simply hand over the receipt to him. In the process, title to the gold has passed from you to him.

Receipts add to the ease of exchange because it is easier to transfer the paper than to transfer the gold itself. But at this important stage in the evolution of the money system, we must remind ourselves of an important point: *it is the gold that is the money; the paper receipts are not money.*

Gold is money because it's a commodity with accepted value and is convenient to use in exchange. The use of warehouse receipts won't change that. All you receive from the warehouse is a piece of paper, acknowledging that there is gold which belongs to you at the warehouse.

Paper could *not* be useful as money because the relative ease with which it is produced makes it inexpensive by nature; you'd

---

1. In case you're wondering if this applies to copper-nickel "coins," we will come to them shortly.

have to use tons of it to obtain the same result served by a few ounces of gold.

The paper takes on value only as it can be exchanged for gold. If the warehouse were to refuse to make the gold available, the receipt would eventually be worthless.

It's similar to storing furniture. You can't sit on a furniture receipt; you can only exchange it for something to sit on.

The paper receipts are not money; they are *money substitutes*. They are receipts that can be readily exchanged for real money.[2]

It is obvious that no one is going to accept a piece of paper just because you want him to. He must be confident that it will eventually bring him what he wants. So there are three essential characteristics required of a worthwhile money substitute, if it is to retain its value:

1. *The warehouse must have a good reputation.* It isn't enough that the recipient trusts the warehouse. It must have general acceptance in the market. Otherwise, the holder of the receipt will be limited to exchanging it for gold; he will not be able to trade the receipt to someone else.

2. *The real money must be readily accessible.* If you could not exchange your receipt for gold any time you wanted to, what lasting value would the receipt have? And that means that . . .

3. *The real money must be kept out of circulation.* If the warehouseman were to spend your gold or lend it to someone else, how could you expect it to be available when you wanted it?

If you hold a receipt, the gold in the warehouse actually belongs to you, not to the warehouse. It would be as preposterous for the warehouseman to use *your* gold as it would be for the Ajax Van & Storage Company to use your furniture while you had it stored there (unless it had your permission).

Imagine, for example, that you walked into a friend's house and found him lying on your sofa. When you expressed your shock, he told you that Ajax had lent him your sofa because it figured you wouldn't be coming back to get it for a year or so.

2. Hereafter, I will use three terms interchangeably: *money substitutes*, *money receipts*, and *paper money*—each meaning receipts that are used in place of real money.

Pieces of paper, as titles to commodities, aren't worth much unless you can exchange them at any time of *your* choosing for the commodity itself.

So to whatever extent any of the three requirements listed above is missing, the money substitute is bound to lose value.

You are paying the warehouseman a fee for a service—the storing of your money. And the gold must be there and accessible for the receipts to have much value.

Along with the normal paper receipts, it is possible to have tokens. A token is a money substitute in metallic form, rather than in paper. The present U. S. copper-nickel tokens are a good example.

These are not coins, since there is no significant inherent value (perhaps two cents worth of metal in a quarter). They are money substitutes. Like paper money, they can only have lasting, constant value if they can be readily exchanged for something of real value.

THE DEVELOPMENT OF CREDIT

If the warehouse shouldn't be lending out money that belongs to its customers, how can credit ever develop?

Easily. Suppose you own some gold that you don't intend to spend for awhile. You agree to lend it to your next-door neighbor in exchange for an extra payment (interest) when he returns the gold. Naturally, you know you won't be able to use the money while it is on loan to your neighbor.

The essential ingredient of *real* credit is that one person *gives up* the use of his money in order to allow someone else to use it. He is paid interest for temporarily getting along without the money.

Warehouses can play an important part in this. The warehouseman can be aware of who needs money and who has it to lend.

For example, you agree to leave a certain sum of gold in the warehouse for a definite period of time—one year, let us say. To compensate you, the warehouse will pay you interest of 3% on your money.

Now that the warehouseman knows you won't demand your money for a year, he can lend it to another customer at 6%

interest—repayable within one year. You have agreed to *give up* the use of the money while the other person has it. You both can't have it to spend at the same time.

In this case, you will not receive a receipt for your gold; because you have no claim upon it for a year. Instead, you will receive a *note* that entitles you to pick up your gold plus the interest at the end of the year.

Here we have the difference between *demand deposits* and *time deposits*. A demand deposit is the storing of your money, for which you *pay* a fee—in exchange for the convenience of using receipts. You can demand your money at any time.

A time deposit is the *giving up* of your money for a specified length of time, for which you *receive* a fee—interest.

And, of course, the warehouse is merely the forerunner of the modern-day bank. The bank is the place where people store their money and where savings are lent out to obtain interest. So let's substitute the word *bank* for warehouse; although it will not change any of the principles involved.

No matter what we call the warehouse, you will produce and exchange only when you believe it will lead ultimately to something you want. You are not going to give up your production or your property in exchange for a piece of paper you think might be worthless. (It *is* possible, of course, to trade for a piece of paper that is becoming worthless without your knowing it.)

If, by now, you've thought to yourself: "My heavens, this is all so painfully obvious," then I'm glad you think so. If what we've seen so far *is* obvious, then it will be easier to see how distorted our present-day monetary structure has become when we examine it later on.

What we're reviewing now *is* obvious—but only in this simplified form. It is not as easy to see these principles amid the complexities of the modern economy, but they still exist.

THE SIZE OF THE MONEY SUPPLY

A number of fallacies have developed regarding the size of the money supply necessary to serve a community.

As with any other commodity, the overproduction of nails or gold or silver (or whatever is the money commodity) will just lessen the value of each unit of that commodity in exchange.

This identifies one element in the setting of prices. Suppose one horse and one cow are approximately equal in general market value. If prices are expressed in terms of gold, then the price of each might be five ounces of gold.

If the money supply were somehow doubled, one horse would still be equal to one cow; but now both of them would be priced at ten ounces of gold. The additional money available would have generated higher bids for the available products and would have caused prices to go up proportionately.

From this we can formulate an equation that shows how the *general price level* of the community is determined.

At any moment in history, there will be a fixed number of goods and services in the market, available for purchase. At the same time, there will be a certain supply of money in the hands of prospective buyers, available to purchase.

All the goods and services will compete against each other for the available money. And all the monies will compete for the available goods and services.

The general price level will be determined by dividing the available goods and services into the available money, creating a formula:

$$\frac{\text{Available Money Supply}}{\text{Available Goods \& Services}} = \text{General Price Level}$$

Or, expressed in a different way,

$$\text{General Price Level} = \text{Money} \div \text{Goods}$$

This is an abstract equation—meaning that its only purpose is to help us visualize what is happening. We could never hope to know the exact amount of money available for purchasing at any given moment; nor is there even any way to measure all the horses and cows and TV repair services in any uniform way.

But the equation serves to show us that *the greater the money supply, the higher prices will be.* Not because a larger money supply makes anything more valuable; but rather because the prices of products are expressed in terms of money. The more money there is, the more will be bid on each item until the supply of available money liquidates the supply of available objects.

This isn't just probable; it's inevitable. If consumers suddenly received gold nuggets that had rained down from heaven, they wouldn't leave prices where they'd been previously. Each consumer would attempt to take advantage of his apparent new wealth to bid more for what he wanted, hoping to bid it away from others.

In the process, prices would invariably go up; the money supply would have increased, but not the available goods and services. No new wealth would have been created (except to whatever extent gold is in demand as a commercial or industrial commodity).

If the money supply decreased, prices would drop. There would not be enough money to buy up the available goods at the old general price level.

Within the general price level, there will be wide variations of prices among commodities as consumers express their preferences. Some prices will even be dropping while others are going up, as consumers change their minds and rearrange the values they have placed on various items.

But the general price index will necessarily result from the amount of money available for spending and the number of objects available for purchase.

CHAPTER 4

What Is Inflation?

$ $ $ $ $

AMERICA IS THE LAND OF OPPORTUNITY. SO I'M GOING TO SUGGEST that you and I go into business together (at least in your imagination, so that I can pose my puzzle to you).

You and I form a partnership, a company that prints counterfeit money. We print 1,000 new $20 bills.

Then we go into San Diego where our affluence (or lack of it) is not known to anyone.

We start spending the bills and are immediately praised by the local merchants and the newspapers. They proclaim that it is a great thing for San Diego that we have come to town, for we're bringing prosperity to a city that was in a recession.

Two weeks later, we leave town with $20,000 worth of goods. The townspeople bid us grateful farewell for all the business we have brought to them.

It's obvious that *we* have benefited from the situation. We traded paper dollars with *no* real value for products that *have* real value.

Assuming that no one ever learns our little secret, has our gain actually hurt anyone else?

In other words, *does anyone ever pay for the benefits gained by counterfeiters?*

Set the book down for as long as it takes to think about that question. Did anyone lose in order for us to gain from our counterfeit spree? And, if so, who?

* * *

What is your answer?

The merchants who received the counterfeit bills did not lose. They could pass the bills on to others for things they wanted. (Part of our assumption was that no one would discover the counterfeiting.)

We gained; the merchants didn't lose. Apparently, no one lost.

But we've overlooked a few people. Not just a few, in fact. *We've overlooked everyone else in the marketplace.* For everyone else will lose in order to make this gain possible.

We can see this easily as we imagine our car leaving San Diego— loaded with goods removed from San Diego's marketplace. We leave San Diego's residents with less property than they had before we came. There will be fewer goods available to divide up among the people there.

In exchange, they received additional paper money that will circulate in the community. But paper money isn't wealth. It simply means there is now *more* paper money to bid for *fewer* goods and services.

Referring back to our price level formula, we see that the general price level is determined by dividing the available goods and services into the available money supply. Since the money supply has gone up and the goods and services have decreased, the result can only be *a higher price level in San Diego.*

The price increase will be irregular. Those who get their hands on the counterfeit money first will gain from it; for they'll have extra spending money, and prices will not have gone up yet. But as that extra paper money passes through the community, it will bid prices upward.

The other people in the marketplace will be paying for our

gain—and *they will do that through the higher prices they pay for each product.*

Let's carry the example a little further. Suppose our arrival and departure were not noticed. In other words, no one was aware that an extra $20,000 was suddenly coming into circulation.

The individual merchants who received our $20 bills would have no reason to suppose that there was anything unusual or temporary about the increase in business. They would simply suppose that their long-standing promotional efforts were finally paying off—that success was on its way at last.

They would most likely hire extra clerks to handle the increased business, maybe order a new sign and a better paint job for the store.

And they would enlarge their inventories to meet the increased demand, of which we appeared to be an example.

But as soon as it became evident that the sudden dose of new business was purely temporary, they would have to retract their expansion plans. They would lay off the extra clerks and cancel the orders for remodeling.

The painter who was to have done the remodeling would, in turn, have to fire his new helpers. And what would he do with all the extra paint he had ordered?

The net result throughout the area would be a state of gloom. Everyone would have extra commitments to pay off and shelves full of undesired stock—all because an illusory boom caused businessmen to gear up to a demand that never really existed.

Would you call that a recession?

But let's not get ahead of ourselves. Instead, let me give you another puzzle to ponder, before we go on.

Suppose I've earned 100 ounces of gold by working in the marketplace. Now that I have it, I decide *not* to spend it. I won't even lend it to someone else or put it in the bank. Instead, I go home and bury the 100 ounces of gold in the backyard.

I steadfastly refuse to spend it. Some of my friends (who are social reformers) come to me and plead with me to spend the money. "After all," they say, "if you spend it, it will provide employment for others."

But I still refuse to spend the money. It remains in a hole in the backyard.

What happens as a result? Is anyone *hurt* by my action? If so, who? Does anyone *gain* from my action? If so, who?

Again, set down the book for as long as it takes to ponder the question.

*   *   *

What is your answer?

The only possible loser in such a case would be *I*—the one who has the money and refuses to spend it. Even then, if I have decided (for whatever reason) that I don't want to spend it, you could hardly say that I am hurt.

But the fact is that I am simply depriving myself. I have produced something in the marketplace that other people now enjoy. The gold I received was my claim to goods and services in the market. When I spend the gold, I am claiming my reward for the things I have already given to others.

If I refuse to exercise that claim, *I* am the loser—for I will have fewer goods and services to enjoy. And, in the process, I will have left that many more goods and services in the market *for others to have*.

This highlights a very popular economic fallacy. Most people believe the market benefits from my *purchase*. But that isn't the case. The market as a whole benefits from my *production*, not my purchase.

When I produce, I add to the total number of goods and services available. When I purchase, I reduce that supply. My purchase is simply the claiming of my reward. If I don't claim it, only I suffer the consequences.

Well then, if I choose to forfeit my reward, who will gain?

Everyone else will profit from my refusal to spend my money.

There will be just that many more goods and services left for the others to split up—since I didn't take my share.

And how will that be reflected in practice?

Prices will be affected by the change in the money supply. As I remove 100 ounces of gold from circulation, prices will drop accordingly (see our price formula). So now everyone can buy *more* goods with the money he already has.

The larger the money supply, the higher prices are. The smaller the money supply, the lower prices are.

ORGANIZED COUNTERFEITING

In a free market, the gold stock would undoubtedly respond easily and quietly to changes in the volume of goods produced. If the available supply of products increased, prices would drop. It would mean each ounce of gold was now more valuable than before, and this in turn would inspire greater production of gold.

On the other hand, if gold were overproduced temporarily, prices would rise and each ounce of gold would be less valuable in exchange. The gold miner would be getting less in return for his efforts. This would discourage production.

Remember that it is *not* the volume of production or the volume of sales that is important to you; it is what you eventually receive for what you have done that counts.

So if gold mining responds smoothly to changes in market needs, the market need never be disrupted by sudden changes in price levels.

However, an intricate economy (like the one in which we live) will use the money substitutes to a much greater degree than the real money. And there is plenty of room for manipulation of the money substitutes. It is possible for new paper money to come into circulation without increasing the production or storage of real money.

And this brings us to the next important element in understanding the money system: *inflation.*

Inflation is an increase in money substitutes above the stock of real money in storage.[1]

Inflation simply means there are more paper money receipts in circulation than there is real money with which to back them up. As we've seen, this will cause prices to go up. But rising prices are not inflation; they are an *effect* of inflation. Rising prices can result from several different causes (decreased production, for example); but only when they result from an overproduction of paper money do they have a lasting effect upon the economy.

It is possible for prices to remain stable or even drop during an inflationary period. This would happen if the production of goods and services increased faster than the increase in paper money (Prices = Money ÷ Goods). *But prices would still be higher than they would have been without the inflation.*

We should note also that the price formula will work in the same way whether the *money supply* element refers to real money (gold or silver) or to money substitutes. An increase in money substitutes will cause prices to go up, even if the stock of real money has remained constant; for the formula is affected by whatever is bid for the available goods and services in the market.

Let us return now to the development of our money system. Suppose you left your gold on demand deposit at the bank (warehouse) and received a receipt that you intended to spend in the marketplace. But the banker didn't store the gold; he lent it to someone else—in order to earn interest on money that isn't his. Or perhaps he just issued a second receipt to someone else.

In either case, two people would be trying to spend the same gold at the same time. You would have *inflation*—two receipts for the same supply of gold.

One consequence of this would be the well-known "run on the

---

1. The definitions used in this book have been created by the author. The purpose of a definition is to establish precise communication between author and reader, not to adhere to any authoritative concept. The worth of a definition comes from its ability to draw a sharp line between what *is* a certain thing and what isn't. There are several definitions of the word "inflation" in popular use; but this one isolates the one factor that has the greatest effect upon general economic conditions.

bank." As soon as anyone became suspicious that the banker was doing this, he'd get jittery about his own money.

"Heavens," he'd say, "if there isn't enough gold in the bank to cover every receipt, then someone will be out of luck if everyone decides to turn in his receipts for gold. That may not happen— but why take a chance? So, even though I'm a public-spirited citizen who doesn't want to undermine confidence in our institutions, I have too many humanitarian projects in mind for my gold. So I'd better run down to the bank and get my gold out while there's still some to get!"

If very many people became suspicious, you'd have a run on the bank. And those who arrived there last would be out of luck— if the bank really were cheating on the receipts. If it weren't, everyone would get his gold and the bank's honesty would be proven. This would probably result in increased business for the bank. An honest bank would not have to fear a run.

But if the banker *is* inflating, and can keep that fact hidden, what then? Obviously, he'll draw extra benefits from his ability to lend out gold that doesn't belong to him.

Who will pay for his benefits? The people in the community will pay the difference in higher prices, resulting from the increase of money substitutes in circulation.

The example is no different from our glorious success in San Diego. The paper money supply has been artificially increased and the people in the marketplace will pay higher prices as a result.

The banker has caused inflation in the same way our counterfeiting hit San Diego.

So let's coin another definition of inflation, one more to the point: *Inflation is the counterfeiting of paper money.*

Inflation is the printing of paper money substitutes that are not backed by real money. And it doesn't matter *who* does the counterfeiting. *Any* increase in paper money—not backed by real money in storage—is going to cause the same reaction: prices will be higher than they would have been without the inflation.

In fact, here's a cartoon that says it clearly:

"I like to think that we're doing our bit to ease the tight money situation."

July 1, 1959
THE WALL STREET JOURNAL

Well, we've already come a long way in the development of our money system. We've seen banks or warehouses storing gold and silver, and issuing receipts for them. (They can even store money substitutes and issue checking accounts as a secondary money substitute.)

We've seen coins minted and circulated. Coins are a form of real money; while tokens are money substitutes.

Lending and borrowing take place as one individual gives up the use of his money for a period of time. This can be done through time deposits in banks.

Any bank that issued more receipts than its stock of real money justified would be constantly vulnerable to a "run" that could put it out of business.

Once those runs became common, individuals would probably

become disenchanted with *all* banks; for how would you know which ones were honest and which weren't? That would put the burden of proof on the honest banks to *prove* their honesty to the satisfaction of their customers. There are many ways by which that could be done, but it isn't necessary to go into them here.[2]

If the banks overprint the receipts and no bank runs take place (so that inflation continues unchecked), then we have seen that prices go up artificially and cause reactions in the marketplace.

We now have all the important elements of a money system at our disposal. So we can leave our island and our warehouses and proceed to modern-day conditions to see what is happening around us.

Our examination of the primitive beginnings of money has been useful to us, however. For it has isolated and identified the principles that exist in any economy. By concentrating on a few elements, we have been able to see them more clearly.

No matter how intricate the economy, no matter how sophisticated "modern economics" may become, some things do not change. For example, *you only produce and exchange when you believe it will lead ultimately to something you want.*

Because of that, actions in the marketplace have reactions, causes have effects, acts produce consequences.

2. For one example, the banks could earmark the gold itself with the number printed on the receipt that goes with it. Anyone could bring his receipt into the bank at any time and be shown the specific gold that backs up that receipt.

CHAPTER 5

The Government and Money

$ $ $ $ $

THE GOVERNMENT EVENTUALLY BECOMES DEEPLY INVOLVED IN ANY economy. It is not our purpose here to examine the merits or demerits of governmental intervention in the economy. What is of immediate concern is the government's involvement in the money supply.

Government inevitably takes over the money system in a country. To understand why this control is so important to government, we need to digress temporarily.

There are three ways for a government to raise the financial resources for its spending activities: taxing, borrowing, and printing.

1. When *taxation* is the method, it's not hard to see that one man's subsidy from the state is another man's tax. The total amount of property in the society hasn't increased; it has only been redistributed according to the government's wishes.

2. If the government *borrows* the funds it spends, nothing changes. Eventually the funds will be due for repayment. That means the taxpayers will pay the bill; or else the loans will be repudiated—which means the lenders pay instead of the taxpayers in general.

We should also notice that, in the short term, the resources the government has borrowed could have been used in the private sector of the economy. These resources have been removed from private use as emphatically as if they had been confiscated through taxation.

Private investment has been curtailed by the amount of the government's borrowings. Two people cannot use the same money at the same time.

3. This brings us to the most subtle method. It is *inflation*. The government, in effect, merely *prints* extra money substitutes and spends them for what it wants.

We have already seen, however, that *these money substitutes only take on purchasing power at the expense of the other money substitutes which are thereby reduced in purchasing power*. Prices are invariably higher than they otherwise would have been.

Just as in our San Diego example, fewer goods and services are available to the rest of the population. The difference is what the government has confiscated through the use of its counterfeit paper money.

No matter how the government covers its spending bills, the end result is that the individuals in the marketplace have paid the cost. Whether government obtains its resources by taxing, borrowing, or printing, the people in general have lost purchasing power to the extent the government has been spending.

But the third method has a highly useful advantage: *few people realize what is going on*. In fact, as prices edge upward, people blame businessmen or the unions for causing what they call "inflation." Actually, it is the government that has taken their resources, but they don't know it. So inflation is the most subtle kind of taxation; it is always attractive to governments.

For example, the government can "benevolently" grant a "tax cut" periodically. But a look at the budget reveals that spending is continuing to increase. How can this be? All that happens, of course, is a shift in emphasis from method one to method three—from taxing to printing.

Whenever the government spends, the people must give up *something*. You can't create something out of nothing.

This brief digression demonstrates why controlling the money system is so important to any government. With this control, it can tax through inflation.

THE INEVITABLE TAKEOVER

Although the details will change from one country to another, we should be able to draw a composite picture of a government moving into a position of control over the money system. This takeover will be in six basic steps.

1. The first step is for *the government to go into the warehouse business,* issuing its own paper money. In no time at all, it succumbs to the temptation of step two.

2. It *prints more receipts than its gold stock justifies.* This, of course, is inflation.

In doing so, however, the government runs into our basic rule of money: you only produce and exchange when you believe it will lead ultimately to something you want.

This means that individuals are not going to accept the government's inflationary money receipts—so long as they can get more valuable receipts from other sources.

3. Eventually this prompts the government to *declare itself to be the monopoly warehouse for gold.* That means no one else may issue receipts for gold. From this point onward, banks are merely storage houses for paper money receipts—since they cannot issue their own receipts.

But our rule still applies; and individuals respond in their own interests by refusing to accept the government's depreciating currency, preferring to use gold and silver.

4. Seeing its receipts refused, the government then *passes a "legal tender law"*—which says that you *must* accept the government's paper money; it is a crime to turn it down when someone offers it to you in payment of a debt or obligation.

If that is to be the case, then most individuals will accept the paper money; but they then turn it in for gold as fast as they receive it. They refuse to hold the paper money for any length of time, preferring to store the gold instead.

The government, however, labels such storing "hoarding." But the rush to turn in the legal tender for gold is nothing more than the traditional run on the bank—only this time it's the *government's* bank.

5. And so, after creating sufficient rationalization for its action, *the government confiscates all the gold*—and declares that henceforth no private citizen may own gold (all this in the "public interest," of course).

The government will store all the gold now (store it, not "hoard" it). And you will use the paper receipts that the government has decreed others must accept from you.

The government can't, however, guarantee what others will give you in return for that paper money—although it may try to do so by invoking price controls.

The confiscation of gold took place in America in 1933. Since then, we have thus been limited to the use of paper money, while the government uses the gold to settle international balances.

6. Along with this, *the government takes control of the banking system.*

The effect of the six-step program has been to confiscate the gold, outlaw all competition in money substitutes, and control the banking system. This is total monetary control.

THE FEDERAL RESERVE SYSTEM

The government's control of the banking system is most important. In modern economics, the banks provide the most effective engine of inflation. So let's turn our attention to the nature of the government's power.

The biggest single step forward in control of the banking system took place in 1913, with the passage of the Federal Reserve Act. All large banks in the nation are members of the Federal Reserve System. Nationally chartered banks are forced to join; state-chartered banks can choose.

The system consists of twelve Reserve Banks, located throughout the country. These twelve Reserve Banks are supervised by the Board of Governors of the Federal Reserve System, who are appointed by the President of the United States.

Some people claim that the Federal Reserve System is a private enterprise. Nothing could be further from the truth. It is as much a part of the government as the Internal Revenue Service, the Commodity Credit Corporation, or the Federal Trade Commission.

The error probably stems from the fact that commercial banks own "stock" in the Reserve Banks. This is not by choice, however; each is forced to put up 6% of its own capital in the nearest Reserve Bank.

Dividends are paid on this; but the dividend is fixed. A commercial bank receives a straight 6% of its investment, not 6% of the Reserve Bank's profits. So the bankers actually only earn 6% on the investment they've been forced to make—not a very exciting return in the banking business.

The remaining profits are turned over to the federal Treasury; and that's where the "big profits" go. Over $7,000,000,000 have been turned over to the government since 1947.

Those profits are not the main interest of the government, however. It is more concerned with using the banks as a method of inflating the money supply. For there are actually three ways of inflating: (1) the printing of receipts, (2) the lending of demand deposits, and (3) the creation of demand deposits.

The first method is the most obvious. The government prints money receipts for which there is no real money as backing. It merely turns on the printing presses—simple counterfeiting.

The second method is only slightly more involved. That method is to take money that is in storage as demand deposits and lend it to someone else. In this way, two people believe they have the use of the same money at the same time. As we've seen, only time deposits can be legitimately lent; for then the owner of the money has agreed to give up his use of the money while it is out on loan.

Demand deposits have evolved into what we call checking accounts, where you withdraw your funds by making a written demand—a check. Time deposits have become savings accounts.

But, as you probably know, anyone can remove his funds from his savings account at any time (despite a technical reservation on your application for a savings account).

As it turns out, then, in both checking and savings accounts, banks are lending out funds that are there purely as storage. No one has agreed to give up the funds for a specified length of time, except in special types of accounts—such as certificates of deposit.

In order to understand the effect of this practice, suppose that you decide to attend an auction. There's a group of vases there that you like. They've been selling at past auctions for about $50 apiece. So you deposit $100 in your checking account, hoping to acquire two vases and pay for them with a check.

The bank, meanwhile, follows its normal practice and lends out $90 of your deposit to someone else.

You arrive at the auction and start bidding. When you bid $50, you expect to have cinched the first vase. But (surprise!) someone across the room bids $60; and so you have to bid higher.

The bidding continues until he bids $90 and you finally bid $100. At that point, he fails to respond and the vase is yours. But a vase you had expected to buy for $50 has cost you $100. So you get only one vase with the money you had expected would buy two.

After the auction, you walk across the room and engage your adversary in conversation. In the process of the conversation, he tells you that he borrowed the money he used to bid against you. In fact, he borrowed it that very morning at your bank.

You discover that *he's been bidding the price up against you with your own money!* The bank has taken your funds, lent them to someone else, and allowed your funds to bid up the price *you* have to pay.

That's a simplified example of how the lending of demand deposits causes inflation.

$ CHAPTER 6 $

How to Create Money

$ $ $ $ $

HAVE YOU EVER BORROWED MONEY AT A BANK? IF SO, THINK BACK to the occasion.

When the loan was approved, did the banker go to the vault, count out the money, and hand you the loan in cash? Probably not. More likely, he handed you a deposit slip, showing that he had credited your checking account with the amount of the loan. If you did not already have a checking account, he probably asked you to open one as a condition of the loan.

In either case, there has been no requirement that currency be available to you. All that was necessary was for him to enter a figure in a ledger, crediting you with x number of dollars. In other words, he may not even have had the cash he lent to you.

But how could a banker do this?

To understand, we need to take a brief look at what is called the *fractional reserve banking system.*

The Federal Reserve System establishes reserve requirements for commercial banks. In recent years, city banks have been required to keep at least 16½% of their checking account deposits on reserve at the nearest Reserve Bank. Rural banks have a lower reserve

requirement: 12½%. Savings account requirements are even
smaller.

To simplify the explanation, we'll concentrate on the city banks.
Any bank in a metropolitan area must keep approximately one-sixth
(16½%) of its checking account deposits at the Reserve Bank.
Suppose, for example, that the bank's records show that its
customers have $100,000 deposited in checking accounts. The bank
must then have at least $16,500 in cash on deposit at the Reserve
Bank.

The superficial purpose of the reserve requirement is to prevent
the bank from lending out so much of its deposits that it would be
highly vulnerable to a run. But, in practice, the result works out to
something quite different.

Since our partnership in the counterfeiting business was so
successful, let's try another venture. This time let's open a bank.

On Monday morning, we open our doors for business for the
first time. The local newspaper carries our advertisement for people
to come in and deposit their funds. The result is that we receive
$1,000 in deposits the first day.

On Tuesday, we advertise for people to come in and borrow
money from us. After all, we intend to make our profits by lending
out the deposits and earning interest.

Since our reserve requirement is 16½%, you would expect that
we would send $165 of our new deposits to the Reserve Bank and
lend out the remaining $835. (We will assume that our operating
expenses are paid out of our initial capital, to avoid complicating
the essential matter involved.)

In that case, our statement would look something like this:

$$\text{Deposits:} \quad \$1,000 \qquad \begin{array}{ll} \text{Loans:} & \$835 \\ \text{Reserves:} & \underline{165 \ (16\tfrac{1}{2}\%)} \\ & \$1,000 \end{array}$$

Our reserve requirement has been met; and we have lent out
$835. That's very simple and easy to understand; but it doesn't
work that way.

For we have the ability to *inflate*—actually to *expand* our
deposits through loans. So it is more likely that we will proceed in

this way: On Monday, we receive $1,000 in new deposits. On Tuesday, we send the *entire* $1,000 to the Reserve Bank as our reserve.

Instead of viewing the $1,000 as our total deposit structure, we will use it as the reserve base and build a much larger deposit structure on top of it.

We then make new loans totaling $5,000—by opening new checking accounts for the borrowers. Whenever anyone asks for a loan, we just add the amount of the loan to his checking account balance. Our statement would then look like this:

> Deposits: $6,000   Loans: $5,000
>
>   Reserves: 1,000 ($16\frac{1}{2}\%$)
>
>   —————
>
> $6,000

In other words, we will accept loan applications; and then grant the loans by issuing deposit slips for money we don't actually have. No one usually asks for currency, anyway—at least not enough people to make a difference.

In the process, we expand our deposits by $5,000 to a total of $6,000. And we have a corresponding figure of $5,000 worth of loans on the other side of the ledger.

Our financial statement balances, our books are in order, and the reserve requirement is being met.

We have just done our bit to ease the tight money situation.

This is the third method of inflation—the *creation* of demand deposits. It is quite similar to the second method—the *lending* of demand deposits.

In fact, method two carried to its logical conclusion becomes the same as method three. Just imagine receiving $1,000 in deposits and lending out $835. The lenders spend their loans and the recipients of the money redeposit the $835 total in our bank. We then lend out five-sixths of that, about $700.

The process is repeated and the $700 is redeposited in the bank. Again, we lend out all but one-sixth, or around $585. And on and on and on *ad infinitum*.

The final result will be that we have loans of $5,000 on the books and a large number of people thinking they have the same

money to spend, thereby bidding up prices. But method three is
much simpler and faster; we just create the new deposits *on top*
of the reserves, as described on the last page.

But there must be a flaw in all this somewhere. Aha! What
happens when the borrowers go out and spend their new checking
account deposits? After all, they're not seeking the loans just to
have funds sitting idly in checking accounts. They have something in mind for those funds. They'll spend them by writing
checks.

Eventually, the town's merchants are going to deposit these
checks in their banks and those banks will come back to our bank
and say, "Give us cash for these checks issued on your bank." What
happens then?

We don't have the cash to give them; we never did. And we'd
be in real trouble at this point, except for one little thing: *the
other banks have been doing the same thing we have.* They've
been inflating their deposits and so we've collected a lot of their
checks, too.

And so our checks are cancelled out by their checks, *provided
we're all inflating at the same rate.* Different-sized banks can
coexist and inflate side by side, so long as the rate of inflation
is the same.

That's the job of the Federal Reserve System—to assure that
uniformity of inflation. It has several tools with which to do this,
the most basic of which is the reserve requirement. With it, the
system controls the volume of inflation in the nation.

CONTROLLING INFLATION

Suppose that the reserve requirement was suddenly lowered
to 14%, or about one-seventh. That would enable us to pyramid
our original $1,000 on reserve at the Reserve Bank still further. We
could now create an *additional* $1,000 in deposits and loans.

Deposits:	$7,000	Loans:	$6,000
		Reserves:	$1,000 (14%)
			$7,000

In other words, $1,000 in reserve will create $5,000 in loans when the reserve rate is 16½%. The same $1,000 in reserve can create $6,000 in loans if the reserve rate is 14%.

The result is a sudden addition to the nominal money supply of the nation. In this way, the Federal Reserve System has the ability to inflate or deflate the paper money supply of the nation, just by changing the bank reserve requirements.

The Reserve Banks also act as the clearing houses between banks, keeping track of the credits one has against the other. If any bank should temporarily be in higher debt than the others, the Reserve Bank can lend it the funds necessary to bail it out.

This process, just described, is *fractional reserve banking*. No matter how much discussion may take place over the raising or lowering of reserve requirements or the efficiency of the operators of the system, the process itself is never challenged publicly. It's become as much a part of the American way of life as high taxes.

The Reserve Banks also issue the currency we use, the green pieces of paper we call *dollars*. They are actually Federal Reserve Notes.

The greenbacks come into circulation as needed. If depositors at commercial banks desire to withdraw more currency, the banks call on the Reserve Banks for extra dollars to meet demands. The Reserve Banks print and issue the currency, as needed, to meet the demands created by a constantly expanding deposit structure.

In modern practice, then, the government does *not* print paper money to *cause* inflation. It prints the paper money *in response* to the inflation that takes place through the bank's deposit-loan expansion.

But the government is still running the show. For the Federal Reserve System determines the extent to which banks may inflate at any given time.

Because of that expansion, all banks are highly vulnerable to runs. So the government has created the Federal Deposit Insurance Corporation to reimburse you for your loss, up to $20,000 on any one account. With this insurance, you aren't supposed to see any reason for withdrawing your funds in shaky times.

"After all, they're as safe as the United States Government."

In reality, the FDIC has nowhere near the funds in reserve to cover any large-scale bank runs. It really only intends to make good by creating new fictitious demand deposits in other banks or by having more paper money printed. In either case, the cure rivals the disease.

THE PAPER MONEY SUPPLY

Before reading this book, you may have assumed that there were greenbacks in the bank vaults for every dollar credited to your checking account. If that were the case, the nation's nominal money supply would simply be the amount of currency that had been printed and issued.

But, as we've seen, that *isn't* the case. There are far more purchasing media than just the greenbacks. People are writing checks for which there is no currency in the bank. The nation's paper money supply is larger than just the currency.

There are really three elements in the supply:

1. Currency outside of banks
2. Checking account deposits
3. Copper-nickel tokens

Any currency inside the bank is probably covered by what has already been credited to checking account deposits. In any event, it is not out in the community bidding up prices. So the only currency we count is that which people hold at home, in their pockets, in cash registers, or elsewhere outside of banks.

The checking account deposits represent immediately spendable money substitutes. They are available to bid up the prices of goods and services in the marketplace.

Tokens that are not silver or gold are not coins, but money substitutes.

The total of these three factors will be the *paper money supply*, the money substitutes that are supposedly backed by the government's gold supply. This also constitutes the *available money supply* in our *general price level* formula. Obviously, this is not *real* money we're talking about. Instead, it is a great deal of inflated paper money, backed up by a small amount of real money.

There are conflicting opinions concerning which elements should be included in the paper money supply. Some economists include savings accounts; others include savings and loan deposits, etc. I'm keeping it as simple as possible here, since what we're looking for does not depend upon a precise figure.

We're also leaving out silver coins. There are so few in circulation that they do not affect prices much. Even the entire amount held by the public would amount to less than 1% of the available paper money supply.

Is there any limit to this paper money supply? The ultimate limits are, of course, the consequences of inflation that we'll examine in the next few pages. There used to be legal limits, also. The law stated that the Federal Reserve System could only issue $140 in currency for each ounce of gold in the Treasury. That law has been repealed.

There was also a law that the reserves of the commercial banks, on deposit at the Reserve Bank, could not exceed four times the Treasury's gold supply, figured at $35 per ounce. That law has been repealed, too.

It's interesting that those who say the 1929 depression couldn't happen again always cite increased "controls" as the reason for their views. But the "controls" are all on private individuals. There are far *fewer* controls on those who generate the inflation than there were in 1929.

And since all these controls have been taken off, it becomes vitally important to understand just what inflation does and where it leads, now that there are no longer any legal limitations upon it.

$ CHAPTER 7 $

Mass Confusion

$ $ $ $ $

EVER WONDER WHY YOUR FAMILY BUDGETS NEVER SEEM TO WORK out as planned? Have you ever wondered why the higher your income goes, the greater the problems you seem to have in just getting by? Oh sure, outwardly you're doing well; but behind the facade there's a constant problem meeting the monthly bills.

Whether or not these specific problems have plagued you, there are a number of somewhat chaotic factors in today's economy. And they make it very difficult to make rational, long-term plans. To see things more clearly requires getting a broader perspective, standing back from the immediate problem.

We've seen that inflation, in the short term, pushes prices upward. Prices are not necessarily higher than they were previously; but they are always higher than they would be without the inflation.

And there will always be a sudden upsurge in demand at the specific points where the inflationary paper money is entering the community. The chief entry points in our economy today are (1) through government spending—defense contracts and subsidies; and (2) through bank loans to businesses and consumers.

The recipients are getting extra paper money that would not have been theirs in the absence of inflation. They respond by gearing production up to a level that didn't exist before. Businessmen order new capital equipment and add workers to the payroll.

In the process, their purchases create new demands on other companies and industries, affecting them in much the same way the inflation recipients have been affected.

It might almost be called a law of nature that *no one ever gets new income without raising expenses accordingly*. Businessmen start offering their suppliers more money to get deliveries faster; and they start bidding workers away from competing companies.

In fact, when a businessman gets a bank loan, he doesn't hire the unemployed. For in reality, there are only two kinds of unemployed: (1) those who don't want to work at prevailing wage levels; and (2) those who are legally prevented from working at prevailing wage levels by the various forms of minimum wage laws and union contracts.

So the businessman gets most of his new workers by bidding them away from other jobs, pushing wages upward.

In the process, the labor unions stage a gigantic show of strength to indicate that *they* are responsible for the higher wage levels, which is not possible. All they can do is to move in and soak up the excess bidding power created by inflation.

If it were not for inflation, any successful union wage hikes would result in unemployment. For the companies involved would be priced out of business by the increased costs. But in an inflationary economy, there is always more paper money in the hands of the company's customers; and that's what makes the so-called wage-price spiral possible.[1]

The two chief characteristics of the inflationary economy are (1) the unrealistic demands created for some companies and in-

1. It is true that inflation, by pushing prices and wages upward, creates the illusion of a higher wage level. That can then induce some of the unemployed to go back to work, thinking (erroneously) that the wage level is now more attractive. It can also push the prevailing levels above the legal minimum wage, freeing some other workers from involuntary unemployment.

dustries, and (2) the constantly rising price level. Our price formula is working, silently but irresistibly; and it applies to prices, wages, everything.

As the paper money flows through the market, it bids prices higher and higher. So those who receive the new inflationary money the soonest will benefit the most; they get to spend it while the lower prices are still in effect.

But as it passes from hand to hand, prices get higher. And some individuals receive it just in time to offset the rising price level and come out even.

Further back down the line are others who receive it too late to break even. And way in the back of the scene are those whose incomes are *not* bid up by inflation. Those are the retired, the pensioners—the individuals who are on fixed incomes that do not adjust upward to inflation, even though prices are going steadily upward.

These individuals in the back of the scene are the ones who are paying for the gains of those getting the handouts from the government and the banks. Every gain received by a handout recipient must be accompanied by a loss to someone else who must now pay more for everything.

Inflation amounts to nothing more than a redistribution of the wealth, a distortion of the purchasing pattern that would have taken place in the free market without inflation. Some people get greater purchasing power at the expense of others whose paper money will no longer buy as much.

And yet, in the short run, inflation *seems* to be producing a "boom." Prosperity *appears* to hit the economy when the government pumps new inflationary paper money into circulation. "After all, you have to admit we never had it so good!"

This is just another example of the visible gain and the hidden loss. The so-called gains from inflation are always spectacular, while the losses are generally hidden from view. So let's go behind the scenes and see the actual sequence of events produced by inflation.

A DAY IN THE LIFE . . .

Each consumer is trying to satisfy his most urgent desires at any given time. He will allocate his limited income on some basis, hoping to maximize his own objectives, whatever they may be.

Let's take a hypothetical engineer, working in an aerospace company. His take-home pay, after taxes, is $800 per month.

Here is an imaginary value scale for this consumer:

$800 Monthly Budget:

1.	Food	$100
2.	Housing	200
3.	Clothing	100
4.	Education	50
5.	Transportation	150
6.	Medical	50
7.	Entertainment	100
8.	Savings	50
		——$800 total
9.	Swimming Pool	100
		——$900 total
10.	Yacht	200
	etc.	

He has certain wants that must be satisfied: food for his family, a house with utilities and other things that go into it, clothing, education for his children, a car or two, medical expenses, and a certain amount of entertainment. With the $50 left over, after taking care of these objectives, he feeds a savings account for the future.

Notice that there are numbers on this imaginary value scale. They are important, because the eight or ten items listed here aren't the *only* things he'd like to have. There are *hundreds* of other things in the world he would love to have, if he only had the money.

As a matter of fact, we can see that he would very much like a swimming pool—but it is just out of his reach. He's also wanted a yacht, but his $800 per month will only go so far. He gets down to item 8 and the budget is used up.

It isn't that he *can't* buy the swimming pool or the yacht. But he's not willing to give up more important things to get them. Instead, he spends an hour or two a day at his desk dreaming of the swimming pool that he knows he can't afford.

But one day the boss calls him into his office to tell him some good news. "Bumstead," he says, "the company has just received a new government contract. That means we can now give you a raise. Your take-home pay is going up by $100 a month."

Naturally, our hypothetical hero isn't concerned with national questions of inflation and the like. All he knows is that someone has finally realized how talented he is and he's been rewarded with a long-overdue raise.

He rushes home, tells his wife, and they spend a good four minutes trying to decide what to do with the raise. They rush out and buy that swimming pool, probably by obligating themselves for the $100 per month the new raise is bringing him.

And the visible effects of his purchase (and the purchases of others like him) produce the appearance of a boom. "Look at all the swimming pools; and people are eating at more expensive restaurants, driving better cars. After all, wouldn't you really rather live in a society where people can afford swimming pools, in addition to the necessities of life?"

There's only one problem. Prices are rushing upward to meet the increased paper money supply caused by inflation—the same inflation that deceived him into thinking he'd received a raise.

And a few months after the raise, he finds that it now costs him $100 per month *more* to live in the same *old* routine than it did before he received the raise.

The raise has been completely absorbed by inflation, as each of the eight most important items on his value scale has gone up in price. It now costs $900 per month to do what previously cost only $800.

The routine he once had has new price tags attached to it. It now looks like this.

$900 Monthly Budget:

1.	Food	$115
2.	Housing	225
3.	Clothing	115
4.	Education	60
5.	Transportation	165
6.	Medical	60
7.	Entertainment	110
8.	Savings	50

$ 900

9.	Swimming Pool	100

$1,000

10.	Yacht	225

etc.

So it would appear that, despite the changes in numbers, his situation has not changed, after all. His income covers the first eight items on the value scale, just as in the old routine.

There's only one problem: *he's not living in the same old routine.* He still has all the old expenses, *plus* a swimming pool that costs him $100 per month. And since no one has yet figured out a way to repossess swimming pools, he now has to eliminate $100 worth of purchases from his monthly budget.

$900 Monthly Budget:

1.	Food	~~$115~~	$105
2.	Housing	225	
3.	Clothing	~~115~~	100
4.	Education	60	
5.	Transportation	165	
6.	Medical	~~60~~	50
7.	Entertainment	~~110~~	60
8.	Savings	~~50~~	35
9.	Swimming Pool	100	

$900

10.	Yacht	225

This means he'll have to go without something he would ordinarily consider a necessity. Changes will have to be made in order to cram the pool into the budget—now that prices have gone up so much.

For as long as it takes to pay off the pool, he'll have to go without some of the things he had always taken for granted. He is now purchasing what he used to, plus a swimming pool, less some things he considered more important than a swimming pool.

What, then, is the net result of inflation on his life? He now purchases approximately *as much* as before; but the *distribution* of his purchases has been artificially altered by the curve he was thrown by inflation.

Had he been given a clear-cut choice, he would never have bought the swimming pool. He would have chosen his former routine, as he did until inflation distorted his decisions. He was always in a position to buy a swimming pool before. All he had to do was to give up something else; but he didn't want to do that. Now his life is less enjoyable because he was temporarily deceived into thinking he could have more than was really possible.

And *he* was one of the first to get the inflationary paper money. Was *his* life improved by inflation?

THE MORNING AFTER

And, of course, what is happening to our hero is also happening to millions of others, in various positions along the handout line. Businessmen are gearing up to these new demands—swimming pools, expensive restaurants, better cars, etc.

But as soon as the inflationary currency has made one complete pass through the market, prices will begin to stabilize again at a new, higher level.

That's the point where the consumers realize that something has gone wrong with their calculations; and they attempt to reassert their old routines. This brings about failures in the glamour industries—swimming pool companies, entertainment, expensive restaurants, etc. But, as we can see, it will also cause slowdowns in the more basic industries, such as food and clothing and housing.

The outward picture is that of the economy passing from a boom stage into a recession. "Too bad, looked as though we really had all-out prosperity for awhile; but now this recession."

During the first stage, businessmen were gearing up to respond to the apparently upgraded tastes of the consumers. We seemed to be entering an era in which everyone would have more.

But the truth of the matter was that nothing had actually changed. We still had the same amount of resources to work with; we still had the same general level of technical competence. But inflation deceived us into redistributing our resources temporarily toward more glamourous industries.

And when the inflationary cycle is over, the businessmen are required to face the fact that they had geared up to a fairy-tale market. Now they must grit their teeth, accept their losses, and resolve not to be fooled again.

Mistakes will have to be liquidated, wasted man-hours written off.

This is a *recession*. Perhaps it is easier to see now what a recession really is. *It is the liquidation period following an inflationary cycle.*

But no government wants the embarrassment of that; and so the money managers look for a way of warding off the recession. And in thousands of years of recorded monetary history, only one temporary solution has ever been discovered. Governments know only *one* way of holding back a recession. What do you suppose it is?

How did you know?

Yes, the only solution they can think of is to *continue the inflation*. The "boom" is *re*generated with more bank credit and government subsidies. Companies appear to come to life again.

Prices go higher, but in such irregular patterns that businessmen and wage-earners are unable to make rational decisions from the distorted price structure.

Inefficient businessmen stay in business with more credit—at the expense of other companies that are offering to satisfy more basic consumer demands.

And, through all this, *the consumer is in a daze.* His concept of his buying power is totally distorted. He sits by his swimming pool, eating a can of beans for dinner. He drives to work in a new car, while his children go without dental care and his furniture falls apart.

Not surprisingly, many individuals begin to think less of themselves, feeling incapable of coping with life in an efficient manner.

The consumer finds himself turning more and more to credit as a means of keeping up with himself. He continually plans ahead, seeing the day when he'll be out of debt. But he never gets there; because his planning is always based upon today's prices and they keep going upward.

Inflation is mass confusion.

No one knows what he is doing. And every man thinks it is *he* who is out of step with the general prosperity.

The businessman, seeing his sales volume larger than ever before, wonders why he isn't showing a profit. It's all he can do to keep his business propped up with bank credit. When he confides in his banker that he thinks he may be a failure, the banker reassures him and grants him a new loan.

The consumer wonders why everyone else is doing so well. He hopes that others will not see how badly he's doing behind the facade of prosperity he has created.

If he could only stand back from his own life, view the entire economy and see what is happening, he would be able to reassure himself of his own sanity. And he would be able to begin taking steps to get out of his predicament.

It is also true that whenever an individual begins to allow for inflation in his calculations, inflation speeds up and manages to stay out in front of him.

CHAPTER 8

Inflation Starts to Gallop

$ $ $ $ $

SO THE GOVERNMENT'S INFLATION DIDN'T PRODUCE PROSPERITY, after all. It simply distorted our choices temporarily.

Why, then, bother to pump inflation into the economy in the first place? Because those who control the inflation (the banks and the government) benefit so much from it. And those who are first in line at the subsidy window are usually the most vocal elements in the market.

The government invokes inflation as a way of appearing to create prosperity; as a way of financing, on a subtle basis, its own programs. Once underway, the inflationary program must be sustained in order to ward off the recession that will inevitably follow.

The additional inflation is simply postponing the day of reckoning. And it is covering up a greater and greater number of miscalculations that must eventually come to light. These mistakes cannot be hidden forever; but the government hopes they can (or at least until another administration is in office).

And so the binge continues, guaranteeing an even *worse* readjustment period ahead. The longer the cycle lasts, the bigger the inflation, the greater number of miscalculations to be liquidated, the worse the recession to come.

But now another element enters the picture. As the money managers attempt to continue the cycle, they find that their doses of inflation don't have the effect they once had. Certainly our anti-hero, Joe Consumer, isn't going to be fooled again by another $100 raise; he's wise now.

But if the next one were to be $150? Ah, that's a different story. "Now I'm *really* getting ahead," he thinks.

It's not that the money managers are consciously aiming to throw our Dagwood Bumstead a curve. They just look at the business trends and become aware of the need for bigger and bigger doses of inflation.

So the subsidy programs get bigger and the bank credit expansion gets more feverish. But, as always, reactions are taking place that were not anticipated.

For example, the government suffers from having to pay higher prices than expected, just as everyone does. Just like us, it plans *its* budget with today's prices in mind; but inflation is pushing those prices upward. So it, too, runs to the bank and borrows to meet a higher-than-expected deficit.

But the paper money won't be there to buy the government's bonds unless the reins on inflation are loosened a little more. So one feeds on the other and vice versa.

At the same time, individuals notice the paper money depreciating rapidly, and they become afraid to hold it. They try to spend it faster. Less savings are available for real credit, creating pressure for phony credit.

And when savings accounts go down, interest rates go up. The government tries to push the rates down by feeding more paper money into the system, hoping to make money more "plentiful."

What we are seeing here are the ways in which the fires of inflation are fanned: (1) bigger spending programs are needed to keep the "boom" from collapsing; (2) unexpectedly higher prices cause the government to borrow more, requiring more inflation to make it possible; and (3) savings accounts become less attractive and consumers spend more; so more inflation appears to be the only way to hold interest rates down.

Each of these things encourages the expansion of inflation at an ever-increasing rate. It multiplies; it doesn't add. One thing feeds on another; and it becomes harder and harder to hold it in check.

When it gets going fast enough, you have *runaway inflation* (or hyper-inflation)—where the paper money is depreciating hourly. And within a short period of time, the entire monetary system collapses.

History is riddled with examples of runaway inflation. It reached such a critical stage during the French Revolution that the state decreed that violations of its legal tender law were guillotine offenses. Yet people *still* refused to accept the worthless currency.[1]

In 1923, Germans were paying a billion marks for a loaf of bread. And there was China at the end of the Second World War; and Brazil and Holland and Indonesia and on and on and on.

Naturally, in each case, the population had been told prior to the crisis that "you never had it so good!"

As Ludwig von Mises has pointed out, the government is the only agency that can take a useful commodity like paper, slap some ink on it, and make it totally worthless.

POISON OR HANGING?

Somewhere along the garden path, the money managers reach a critical junction. After having inflated steadily, they reach a point where all the many alternatives that were once available have disappeared. There are only two dismal alternatives left.

One choice is to continue inflating. But by this point, it has gone too far. Further inflation means they'll lose control completely and runaway inflation will take over.

But the only other alternative is to stop the inflation. And that

1. An excellent case history of runaway inflation is provided in Andrew Dickson White's *Fiat Money Inflation in France.*

will bring to light all the miscalculations of the past. It means an embarrassing liquidation period ahead. Only it won't be just a recession. Now inflation has gone so far that the readjustment period will be a full-scale depression, with widespread business failures, unemployment, and bank closings.

In fact, at this point, it doesn't require a deflation (removal of paper money from circulation) in order to cause a recession. It doesn't even require an end to currency expansion. All that's necessary is to just *slow down the rate of increase.* Once you've gone far enough, that's all it takes to bring on the depression.

So this is now their choice: runaway inflation or depression. The money managers may not even be aware of the fact that they have arrived at that juncture. They may go right on inflating, unaware of the consequences. But once they have reached that fork in the road, it is far too late to turn back and correct their mistakes.

THE GOLD DRAIN

While all this is going on, the money managers are also fighting on another front.

Inflation makes many people jittery about the future of the currency. And so those who can turn in their dollars for gold (mainly foreign banks and governments) do so, as they see the value of the dollar rapidly sliding downward.

The gap between the gold supply and the money substitute volume reaches a point where a run on the gold seems inevitable. And no one likes to be last in line at a run.

Preserving the remaining gold becomes a national problem. Such things as "balance of payments" become important issues. Attempts are made to keep American citizens from enhancing their lives by buying attractive foreign goods.

It's interesting to note that, without inflation, there would never be any such thing as a "balance of payments" problem. Every dollar that could be spent (and eventually turned in to the Treasury) would have gold to back it up. Foreign trade would be encouraged as a way of widening our choices.

But with inflation, it's a big problem. And the government watches its gold supply getting smaller and smaller, until the situation becomes desperate. Here, too, a juncture is finally reached where there are only two alternatives left.

One obvious alternative is *deflation*—withdraw some of the excess paper money from circulation. That would close the gap between the gold supply and the volume of outstanding money substitutes, reducing the overwhelming demands on the gold stock.

But that means being prepared for the depression that would certainly follow. And if you wait too long to deflate, it can be too late. At that point, the run on the gold may have started. A short-term answer to the crisis is needed, and deflation would not work fast enough.

The second alternative is not widely understood. The government simply *defaults* on its agreement to redeem dollars with a stated amount of gold. Only it isn't called a default; it is called a *devaluation*.

The government has promised, in effect, to pay out one ounce of gold for every 35 dollars turned in at the Treasury. Surveying the situation, the government sees that outstanding claims against the gold stock are perhaps six times as great as the gold supply itself.

And perhaps it calculates that about half of those claims are in the hands of people in a position to exercise them. So the government finally decides that it has no alternative but to change the rules in the middle of the game.

After having issued the dollars on the basis of a fixed rate of exchange, it now changes the rate. It says that it will no longer redeem one ounce of gold for every 35 dollars turned in. Now it will pay out only *one-half ounce* for every 35 dollars. In other words, it will take 70 dollars, instead of 35, to claim one ounce.

This is a *devaluation: a repudiation of the government's promise to honor its money substitutes at the stated rate of exchange.*

It is important to recognize exactly what a devaluation is. It is not a mere adjustment of exchange rates; it is not a raising of the price of gold. It is a default on a debt.

It is a bankrupt debtor deciding to pay off his debts at 50 cents on the dollar (or any other percentage chosen).

A 50% devaluation would mean changing the redemption rate from $35 per ounce to $70 per ounce, cutting the dollar's redemption value in half. A 67% devaluation would mean changing the redemption rate to $105 per ounce.

A 100% devaluation would mean refusing to redeem any gold at all. That is what American citizens suffered in 1933. Since then, no American has been legally permitted to own gold bullion or any gold coins dated later than 1933.

When a government devalues its currency, its seems to have solved the problem. For devaluation will seem to take the pressure off its gold supply for awhile. Inevitably, this encourages more inflation; the consequences *seem* to have been eliminated, at least temporarily.

Before the devaluation, there are many stop-gap measures a government may invoke, attempting to delay the inevitable. Most of these involve a false show of confidence in the future of the gold supply, hoping to dissuade foreign creditors from collecting their gold.

So the government ponders the dilemma of *deflation or devaluation* in trying to save its gold stock. And back on the other front, it's the dilemma of *runaway inflation or depression*.

Each of these problems becomes more and more aggravated, even while the government displays its most confident posture to the world.

And we hear more and more about the "new age" of monetary matters, the "archaic reliance on gold," the gold speculators who are pictured as the villains, and other fictions that are intended to draw attention away from the *real* problem, the problem no one wants to end: *inflation*.

All of the tricks up the government's sleeve have been tried before and have failed to avert the inevitable. But that won't stop it from trying again.

CHAPTER 9

Who Will Protect You?

$ $ $ $ $

HOW MANY TIMES HAVE YOU HEARD A STATEMENT LIKE THIS: "We could never have another great depression in this country; the government has the power now to intervene and prevent such things from happening"?

In the first chapter of this book, we saw that there was no shortage of governmental powers in 1929. Still, there was a depression. It is very instructive to review the events of the 1920s and 1930s. They represent the classic example of the inflation-depression cycle we've been examining in this book.

Anyone who believes that America of the 1920s was an example of unregulated free enterprise has not checked history very closely. As noted before, I recommend Murray Rothbard's outstanding book, *America's Great Depression*, as the most thorough economic history of the period 1921–1933.

In Rothbard's book, I counted 43 major federal activities in operation during the "Roaring Twenties." Here are some of those programs:

1. The Federal Reserve System launched a full-scale bank inflation during the twenties. By controlling the reserve requirements, it gave banks the lending power to create new paper

money. In addition, in 1923, the Reserve Banks began purchasing government bonds in the open market to facilitate deficit spending and to add to the paper money supply.

Prices could have been lowered during the twenties; it was a period of high production. But it became apparent that the Federal Reserve Board was following a policy aimed at stabilizing prices. Later, John Maynard Keynes hailed "the successful management of the dollar by the Federal Reserve Board from 1923 to 1928 . . . ."

2. Meanwhile, the New York Federal Reserve Bank extended credit directly to the Bank of England to help offset the damage done by the British inflation (just as it did during the sixties). Similar credits were extended to the central banks of Belgium, Poland, and Italy.

3. In August 1921, Congress authorized one billion dollars in credits to the War Finance Corporation, to be lent directly to farmers' cooperatives and foreign importers of American farm goods. The purposes of the bill were to raise farm prices, provide cheap credit to farmers, and increase farm exports. There hasn't been a free market in agriculture since then.

4. During the First World War, the government seized the railroads. They were finally returned to their owners in 1920. But in 1926, the Railway Labor Act was passed. This imposed upon the railroads the same sort of regulation that the National Labor Relations Act later brought to the rest of American industry.

5. Federal taxing policies were used to influence activity in the stock market. In addition, the futures markets were regulated as a result of the Capper Grain Futures Act and the Futures Trading Act.

6. Business regulation started with the signing of the Constitution and its provisions for tariffs and interstate commerce laws. But it was greatly heightened by the anti-trust legislation passed at the turn of the century, plus the establishment of the Federal Trade Commission, the Interstate Commerce Commission, etc.

So please don't delude yourself by looking to the government for the way to avoid the inevitable consequences of inflation. That's confusing the cause of the problem with the solution.

There has never been any shortage of governmental intervention in the economy. But those who say, "We won't have a rerun of 1929 because the government has more power to intervene," are actually correct. The government *does* have more power; and so we will not have a rerun of 1929.

We will have something more severe.

In general, American depressions have been getting steadily worse. As the government develops more "sophisticated" techniques for prolonging inflationary cycles, it causes more painful liquidation periods.

INFLATION IN THE TWENTIES

The seeds of the 1929 depression were planted in the First World War and the inflation that accompanied it. After the war, some of the paper money was cleared out, causing the recession of 1921.

Then the state embarked upon a full-scale inflationary cycle lasting through 1928, at which point money substitutes outnumbered the real money by a ratio of eight to one.

PAPER MONEY SUPPLY
(December 31, 1928)

Checking Account Deposits	$23.1 billion
Currency in Circulation:	3.6 billion
Total Money Substitutes:	$26.7 billion
Gold Stock (real money):	$3.0 billion

The big problem facing the money managers in late 1928 was the heavy demand to redeem gold, coming from both Americans and foreigners. The Federal Reserve Board chose to meet the issue by deflation, rather than by devaluation. The inflationary cycle ended and the inevitable miscalculations started coming to light.

THE STOCK MARKET

It's important to realize that the stock market, like everything else in the economy, displays the effects of inflation. In fact, it's a particularly sensitive indicator of paper money in circulation because of its liquidity, its constantly moving price structure.

The stock market not only responds to inflation; it also benefits from it. It is like the swimming pool industry. It's an ideal investment receptacle for people who have been led to believe they have more money than they really do. In an inflationary cycle, many people who have no business investing are led to believe they have the funds to do so.

This pushes stock prices up faster than the general price rise. Other people, viewing the stock market from outside, see it as a way to beat the depreciation of the dollar. They withdraw their savings from banks and savings banks, and buy stocks instead.

The availability of margin credit adds to the number of people betting on higher stock prices. But margin credit is not the culprit of the stock market orgies. The villain is inflation. Without inflation, there wouldn't be the feeling that higher prices are inevitable. People would not be so anxious to use margin if there was a good chance the stock price might drop; for losses are greater if the falling stock is margined.

In addition, the paper money needed for margin loans wouldn't be available without inflation.

The new paper money flowing into the stock market bids the prices of stocks well beyond the levels justified by any prosperity the companies involved are experiencing. And we see the spectacle of stocks selling at 30 to 100 times their earning values.

At that point, the stock market moves by *psychology* rather than fundamentals. It is no longer a question of what a particular *company* is likely to do in the future. The question is: what will *other speculators* think the *stock* of that company will do?

Chartists take over the market, looking for statistical trends, "break-outs," and other phenomena of *mass psychology*. The real fundamentals are ignored: supply and demand, company profits, markets, management, etc.

But when the inflation ends, the stock market begins to drop— *inevitably*. It *has* to drop because there is no paper money to support the higher price level.

All during 1929, people in the stock market fought to push the market to higher levels. They succeeded temporarily, despite the deflation beginning around them. But the break had to come. By October, the point had been reached where it was literally impossible to support the old price levels; the paper money just didn't exist any more.

The panic on October 29 was not the cause of the depression, nor even the advent of it. It was simply the irrefutable signal that there was a depression in progress—that the dream world had ended. The price was about to be paid for years of tinkering with the money supply.

All speculative orgies are the result of inflation. Neither stock booms nor land booms could be sustained without inflation. There just aren't the resources available for people to buy-at-any-price unless inflation is pouring paper money into the economy. And the booms always collapse when the inflation ends.

THE DEPRESSION BEGINS

Surprisingly, once the inflationary cycle ends, there doesn't have to be widespread misery. The greatest losers will be the businessmen who have large sums of capital tied up in production facilities and inventories that are not needed.

With the inflation over, prices and wages will drop to whatever realistic points are required to get things moving again. Unwanted inventories will move at *some* price; and workers can be employed at *some* wage. No matter what the state of the economy, there are an infinite number of unsatisfied human desires; thus, there is always a market for someone to work to satisfy them.

But what distinguishes a painful depression from a mild recession is the inability to get it over with. If the government has enough control over the economy, it will usually use that power to *prevent* wages and prices from falling to their natural levels. For some strange reason, high prices and high wages are assumed to be symptoms of a healthy economy—whereas they are only symptoms of inflation.

And so everything is done to hold the price level up, even

though it is not possible to trade at those higher prices. And, in the process, the economy comes to a dead halt. You can't live in a world of high price levels when there is no longer paper money to support those levels.

The 1929 depression evoked the ultimate in governmental interference. Herbert Hoover has been characterized so often as a "do nothing" President and the symbol of the "rugged individualist." But that isn't true. He reacted to the depression by calling for a fantastic program to keep wages and prices high, and to prevent the liquidation of mistakes.

He vowed to reverse all previous governmental policies in fighting this depression. And he did. In the process, he succeeded in keeping the economy immobilized.

When Franklin Roosevelt ran against Hoover in 1932, he castigated the President for his big-government techniques. He promised to cut the size of government and to let free enterprise make its way out of the depression unhampered.

Naturally, that never happened. Politicians only call for the reduction of powers they don't hold themselves. Governors, in general, are for states' "rights." Presidents are for federal "rights." If you want to change a governor's attitude toward federal power, make him President.

Roosevelt decided on a different policy from that pursued by Hoover, however. He was anxious to get the engine of inflation going again. But there was still that strain on the gold stock.

So he removed the pressure by prohibiting Americans from owning gold (a 100% devaluation), and then devalued the dollar by 41% for foreigners.

This gave him clear sailing to inflate with a vengeance. And he did.

But he continued to force wage and price levels as high as possible, and they managed to stay ahead of the inflationary push. So nothing happened. At the end of the thirties, there was still no improvement. And by that time, the economy was tied up in red tape.

Finally, the preparation for war created an all-out inflation that broke the price-fixing logjam, and things began to move.

Since then, we've been on one long inflationary spree. Each attempt to slow down the cycle has been met with a recession and a quick return to more inflation. The mistakes being piled up are enormous; and the problem has reached far greater dimensions than those that existed in 1929.

The next time you read that we're in the longest sustained "boom" in American history, you must remind yourself that, unfortunately, this means we're awaiting the worst depression yet.

The boom is unreal; but that doesn't mean that all the prosperity is. America's great productive strength has grown steadily since the industrial revolution. It's the growth in technical proficiency that has brought us prosperity. That growth is the only meaningful kind of progress in the real world. To whatever extent there is inflation, to that extent the prosperity is *diminished*.

How can one believe that the hundreds of billions of dollars spent on wars and foreign aid and welfare can possibly produce prosperity? That capital and energy and time could have gone into building things that actually improved our standard of living. Instead, the resources have been diverted into non-productive enterprises that reduced what we would have had otherwise.

It staggers the mind to wonder what we would be enjoying today if we had not lost so much of our productivity to wasteful endeavors encouraged by the inflationary cycle.

How far has that cycle gone? Here is the scorecard.

PAPER MONEY SUPPLY
(December 31, 1969)

Checking Account Deposits:	$212.9 billion
Currency in Circulation:	46.3 billion
Total Money Substitutes:	259.2 billion
Gold Stock (real money):	$10.4 billion

(Source: Federal Reserve System)

The inflationary ratio was eight to one in 1928. Now it is 25 to one. The money substitutes are 25 times the gold stock backing them up.

These are mere figures and I know of no magic formula that attaches any particular significance to any particular ratio. But we can see that in just the last 12 years the ratio has changed its direction, when plotted on a graph. It would be hard to believe that we aren't getting very close to the runaway inflation stage.

It's most important to recognize that there *is* a problem. All the clichés in the world won't solve it.

We are told that all we need is confidence. But confidence in what? Confidence that the immutable laws of economics have been repealed? Confidence that the world is going to start spinning in the opposite direction from now on? Confidence that acts no longer have consequences?

Can a man falling from a 30-story window, pulled toward the ground by gravity, solve his problem with confidence?

We are told that we don't need gold. "After all, the dollar is backed by the tremendous productive capacity of the nation." That sounds great—until you examine it a little more closely. For what is being said is that the government must have the right to confiscate your production to back up its currency.

The currency and the economy are two different things. The government is wholly responsible for the currency it issues. We, as individual human beings, are responsible for the productive capacity. If you'd like to pledge your wealth, your resources, and your production as the backing for the government's currency, you're welcome to.

Money is a commodity that is accepted in exchange. It is not a hope, not an abstraction, not a measure of production, not a short-term note. It is a commodity that individual human beings are willing to hold while waiting to make purchases.

No one will produce or exchange unless he believes it will lead ultimately to something he wants.

You can't impose a valueless money system upon people and expect that there won't be reactions. Gold and silver evolved as

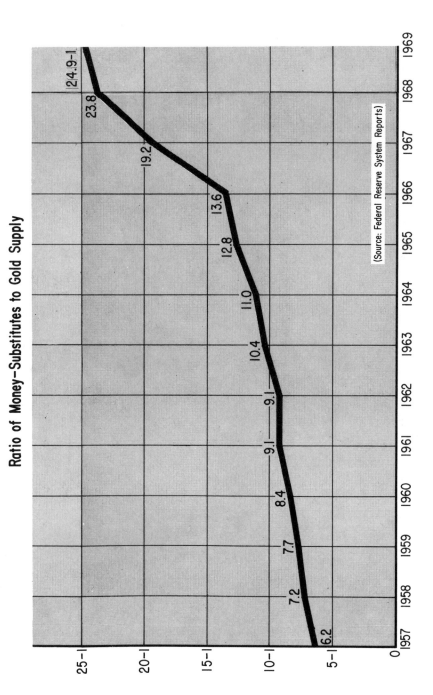

Ratio of Money-Substitutes to Gold Supply

(Source: Federal Reserve System Reports)

money commodites out of billions and billions of human exchanges. They will not be superseded within our lifetimes. Governments can reject them, but individuals will continue to use them.

That won't stop government officials from looking for ways to replace gold, however. But there is no way out of their dilemma. Special Drawing Rights are not the answer. World currencies are not the answer. "Paper Gold" is not the answer. There is no answer, because the money managers don't even understand the question.

Governments don't like gold because it tells them when they do wrong things. Without the gold, they might be able to stretch their misdeeds a little further.

But it will not stop the consequences. They're inevitable.

You can't build a monetary system on sand and expect anything but dire consequences.

And that's exactly what we have today—a system that is based upon a commodity with no inherent value.

ADVANTAGES OF GOLD & SILVER AS MONEY:	ADVANTAGES OF PAPER AS MONEY:
1. Durable	1.
2. Divisible	2.
3. Convenient	3.
4. Consistent	4.
5. Accepted Value	5.

$ CHAPTER 10 $

What Lies Ahead?

$ $ $ $ $

MOST INDIVIDUALS, AT SOME POINT IN LIFE, COME TO REALIZE THAT there are certain cause-and-effect relationships that exist in this world.

If you hold this book out in front of you and let go of it, it will fall toward the floor. That's not just possible, or even probable; it is inevitable. That's because there are certain natural laws that exist. And all the wishing in the world will not change them.

The same is true in economics, although this is not as widely realized. There are certain laws of human nature that translate themselves into inflexible economic cause-and-effect relationships that cannot be denied or overruled.

The possibility of free will in human beings doesn't change their happiness-seeking natures. As a result, there are certain overall responses that are inevitable.

Our simple rule is a good example of this: *You only produce and exchange when you believe it will lead ultimately to something you want.* The rare instances that appear to be exceptions to this rule are not really exceptions. It is just that, in some cases, we (as outsiders) don't happen to know what it is that the individual wants. So it appears to us that he is not directing his efforts toward what he wants.

There are also many instances where an individual knows what he wants but, through ignorance, does not do what is necessary to get it. We have seen that a man produces or exchanges only in order to get what he wants. This prompts him to avoid being paid for his efforts with paper money that is worthless.

But what if he *doesn't know* that it's worthless? Suppose it is paper money that he has believed in since he was old enough to know what it is?

In that case, he may very well take actions that are dangerous to himself, unknowingly. The millions of individuals who lost savings in banks in 1933 were not acting against their own interests. They had been led to believe the banks would never close their doors.

Today, those who believe that the dollar is perfectly sound are not masochists. They are just not interested in finding out for themselves the truth of the situation. As a result, they will continue to tie up their assets in investments that are vulnerable to a sick dollar.

But none of this changes the inexorable laws of economics. They continue to move irresistibly to destroy those who violate them. All acts have consequences; and there's no way to avoid them.

One outgrowth of our basic rule is an economic principle called Gresham's Law. It says, in essence, bad money drives good money out of circulation. In other words, if an individual holds two types of money, of unequal value, he will spend the bad money and save the good money.

The operation of Gresham's Law does not depend upon every individual being an economic genius. It happens anyway.

A good example of this took place in the United States during 1964 and 1965. The dollar was continuing to depreciate rapidly. American citizens couldn't legally own gold. But silver coins were available.

At that time, the value of the silver in a silver coin was slightly *less* than the face value of the coin (a silver quarter had about 23¢

worth of silver in it). But the silver had value; the paper was intrinsically worthless.

Consequently, the silver coins began to get scarce. Pretty soon it became almost impossible to keep the cash register stocked with dimes, quarters, or half-dollars. It reached a point where the government (after having tried to flood the market with 300 million ounces of new silver coins) gave up and switched to copper-nickel tokens.

Did everyone have to understand economics for this to happen? No. Enough individuals were uneasy about the future of the dollar; and they turned to the only alternative they could see. Some persons may have been doing the exact opposite of what Gresham's Law indicates; but the overall effect in the market was a perfect example of economic principle in action.

Because of the great number of people involved, and the differing levels of understanding, Gresham's Law cannot tell us how soon a given reaction will occur. It is a bad mistake to take a general principle and try to predict specific short-term market activity from it. You have no way of knowing the thinking of every individual who may be involved.

We live in an uncertain world; there is no way to obtain absolute knowledge of every causal factor. So exact predictions are out of order. But that doesn't change the inevitability of certain consequences. We know those consequences will come because the acts that cause them have already been committed.

WHAT IS POSSIBLE?

In the past few chapters, we have seen that the government's actions have narrowed the future to a handful of alternatives. There are many things that might have been possible 20 years ago but cannot happen now (at least not until this cycle has run its full course).

We have seen that after inflation has gone far enough (and it has), the alternatives are narrowed to either *runaway inflation* or a full-scale *depression*.

And we've seen that, in order to save the gold supply, there are only two possible choices: *deflation or devaluation*. Recognize that an outright rejection of gold, demonetization, is simply a 100% devaluation.

Since the inflationary cycle has long since passed the point where other courses of action might have been possible, we can concentrate on four possibilities. And we can see that they fall into four potential sequences of events. Henceforward, we will have to travel one of four possible roads:

Sequence #1: Continued inflation—deflation—depression. This sequence begins where we are now—with the inflationary cycle continuing. Then the government begins deflating (or its equivalent, a slowdown in the growth of inflation). The deflation starts the liquidation period and a depression is on.

Sequence #2: Continued inflation—runaway inflation—depression. In this sequence, the government refuses to let up until it's too late and runaway inflation hits. The aftermath of runaway inflation is a depression, but a different kind of depression. We'll see the difference a little further along.

Sequence #3: Continued inflation—devaluation—more inflation—deflation—depression. This sequence includes a devaluation as a way of preserving the gold supply. But since that does not solve the problem, eventually the government is back to the depression–runaway inflation choice again. And this sequence presupposes that it will choose the depression road when that juncture comes.

Sequence #4: Continued inflation—devaluation— more inflation—runaway inflation—depression. This sequence is the alternative to number three. In this one, after devaluing the dollar, the government lets inflation expand until it becomes runaway inflation.

We have not isolated short-term recessions in this sequence. Actually, they're a part of continued inflation. There will be attempts by the money managers to pull in the reins slightly and then let them out again, hoping to perpetuate the cycle that way.

Thus any period marked *inflation* in the sequences can include short-term recessions. Whether or not they happen, and how many there will be, depends upon the length of time inflation continues before becoming another stage.

That length of time could be one more day or it could be a matter of another year or so.

But every one of these sequences ends in a depression of one kind or another. There is nothing that can avert it—not a devaluation or runaway inflation or world currencies—nothing. You cannot have large-scale inflation without large-scale depression. We've already had the first, so it's just a matter of time until we get the second.

This does not have to be depressing to *you*. Once you recognize the inevitability of it, you can take steps to be sure it doesn't destroy *your* life.

Some may say there should be a fifth sequence. That would consist of only one element, which we could call an *economic miracle*. In that case, there would be no more inflation, but no depression either, no devaluation, no runaway inflation—just bliss. In other words, prosperity from this point forward, without any more inflation.

Impossible as that may seem by now, I believe that was what President Nixon promised.

It isn't that a world without depressions is impossible. It is simply too late to try to make that happen now, after 30 continuous years of inflation.[1]

Meanwhile, we can see four possible sequences of events. There is no way to know for sure which of the four we shall get. But by recognizing the various elements involved in the sequences, and by protecting yourself properly, you do not have to know *exactly* how the future will unfold.

It is not difficult, as you will see, to protect yourself adequately against all of these possible sequences.

So let's take the sequences apart and list all of the possible events that could take place—without regard for sequence.

---

1. If the *economic miracle* should happen, I promise to write another book to show you how to make out in good times.

Possibilities:

Continued inflation
Short-term recession
Depression
Runaway inflation
Devaluation

It is necessary to face up to each of these possibilities and know what will happen in the event of each. Then you can make sure that you are not vulnerable.

There are many common misconceptions about each of these; so we shall take a close look at them in this and the next two chapters.

CONTINUED INFLATION

Continued inflation means a continuation of the *status quo*, no change in present conditions.

But that isn't really possible. The only way the money managers can keep the cycle going is to increase the tempo. We've already seen (in the chart on page 69) that this has been happening.

And since all-out inflation will lead too easily to runaway inflation, the only hope for maintaining the cycle is to create larger and more frequent expansions and contractions in the paper money supply. There will be more frequent changes in the tempo— more inflation, then a slight deflation, and more inflation.

The mass confusion that already exists will get much worse. You will find it more and more difficult to make rational decisions in business, investments, purchasing. The pricing structure will become more distorted.

Even if you assume that the present cycle will continue for some time yet, it won't really be the same as it has been. It will get more confusing.

It is conceivable that the present cycle could last through 1971, although that is not too likely. But if you bet that it is going to, and you arrange your investments accordingly, you will be burdened with tension and anxiety in the meantime, afraid that the ax may fall too soon.

If there is some time left, by all means use it to get your house in order. Get rid of all of your vulnerabilities; invest in the things that will make a profit from the coming events. Then you can relax and enjoy the rest of the time available before the crisis comes.

Adjust to the present by recognizing that you are living in the middle of confusion. Don't jump at the normal signals. If your income suddenly goes up, don't respond the way our anti-hero did. Treat it as a pure windfall—something that may not last.

Use the added funds to pay off debts or to make some of the investments that will be recommended in this book. Under no circumstances should you use any new income to obligate yourself to any lasting commitment, such as a time payment contract. If nothing else, just spend the money on yourself as you get it; but spend it as you get it, not in advance.

SHORT-TERM RECESSION

If the inflationary cycle continues much longer, there will necessarily be short-term recessions as a part of it. Inflation relies upon confusion. When the confusion ends, the "boom" is over. And heavy in-and-out breathing of the paper money supply will create a boomlet-recession pattern that will sustain the confusion, at least for awhile longer.

Once any recession begins, the money managers won't want it to go very far, plunging us into a depression. The only way to prevent that will be to quickly step up the inflationary pressure, causing more miscalculations and preventing any liquidation process from beginning.

The significant result of this is *there will be no real drop in the general price level.* Traditionally, a recession is a time to have a strong cash position, to buy at lower prices. But that won't be the case; prices will not have time to drop. The only exception might be some companies that are actually bounced all the way out of business. They might be the sources of disaster sales. But that will be exceptional.

The temporary readjustment period will create price drops and loss of sales in inflation-aided businesses and investments, however. The stock market, real estate, and other investments will suffer.

Otherwise, the main effects of the short-term recession will be temporary discomfort, heightened confusion, and then back on the inflation trail again.

But if the money managers flub their timing, the recession could become a depression before they realize it. In that case, we have an entirely different set of circumstances.

CHAPTER 11

Depression or Runaway Inflation?

$ $ $ $ $

YOU MAY HAVE HEARD THE OLD GAG ABOUT THE DIFFERENCE between a recession and a depression. A recession is when the man next door is out of work. A depression is when *you're* out of work.

Such a definition may be to the point, but it doesn't quite suffice for our purposes here. But what *is* a depression? What are the conditions that must exist to turn a recession into a depression?

Obviously, such a thing can be defined in any way that is useful to the person doing the defining. But I think you may find my definition helpful; so let's review a few points from chapter nine.

When deflation sets in, the general price level starts falling, because paper money is being removed from circulation.

If there were no artificial restraints, wages and prices would fall freely until it became profitable to hire people at the new, lower wage rates. And products could be purchased, even though less paper money existed.

Even economically illiterate individuals would be forced by necessity to lower their asking prices until they obtained jobs.

A man who used to make three dollars an hour might not like the idea of working for one dollar an hour. But once having done so, he would find that he could buy much more than he had expected. Other wages and prices would have fallen, too. Most people would not suffer from the falling prices.

If the economy were free to allow liquidations to take place, the liquidation period would be relatively short and not everyone would suffer. The worst burdens would fall on those who had made the worst business calculations and on those who had mortgaged themselves too heavily at higher price levels.

But governments never seem to want to leave bad enough alone. They intervene to force wages and prices to stay at their previous high levels. Rather, we should say they force *asking* prices and wages up. But with no paper money available to support those high wages and prices, the results are unemployment and unsold goods.

The government also tries to bring "relief" to the economy by preventing the liquidations that would cleanse the market of its problems. Resources continue to be squandered on those businesses that the economy can't afford.

And so a short-term recession becomes a long-term depression. Here's the difference: A *depression is a liquidation period in which governmental restraint of trade prevents orderly liquidation, thereby prolonging a recession.*

In late 1928, the Federal Reserve System stopped the inflation cycle and the recession began. When panic hit the stock market the following October, the government stepped in with both feet. It did everything possible to hold prices and wages up—and it was fairly successful.

Meanwhile, the deflation continued; and the two contradictory forces produced an economic standstill. The government wanted to begin inflating again. But the gold supply was in jeopardy; and that was what had prompted the deflation to begin with.

When Roosevelt replaced Hoover, he decided to take the pressure off the gold stock by devaluing the dollar. He then felt at liberty to start inflating. But it wasn't until the end of the decade that the inflation finally raised the general price level above the artificial minimums imposed by the government and the newly armed labor unions.

President Hoover arrogated to himself a great many new powers with which to "fight the depression." But in the perspective of history, he *does* look like a "do-nothing" President when his administration is compared with the overhaul that Roosevelt engineered.

Since then, the trend toward bigger and bigger government has continued unabated. No administration has reversed it and no administration is likely ever even to try. This means the government's ability to bring the economy to a standstill has multiplied since the thirties.

As a result, it would be a grave mistake to act upon the assumption that the next depression will be a rerun of 1929. The government has far greater control over the economy now. And that means the liquidation will be much more difficult, if not impossible.

But we can't stop there. The last depression was a catalyst for great changes in the relationship of government to the people. It would be foolish to think that the next depression won't be the same.

In 1928, many Americans complained that the federal government had too much power, that it spent too much money on public works and farm programs, and that it was generally tending toward "socialism." But how many of these people would have thought that within six years it would be illegal for an American citizen to own gold?

How many Americans, while voting the bureaucratic Hoover out of office in 1932, would have believed there could be a network of federal agencies like the NLRB, the SEC, etc., within four years?

And it is just as difficult now to project the present trend into the future and see what tomorrow's "enlightened" government may have in store for us. For example, I would not be surprised to see wages frozen at current levels, by presidential order.

We've seen already that party labels are no protection.

If there is to be a miracle, it may be that the President who faces the next depression (probably Richard Nixon) will be more economically astute than his predecessors. If he were to fight the depression by lifting the present governmental controls on the economy, he would be performing that miracle—and the depression would be much shorter and less painful. But how much chance is there of that?

It would be far more realistic to assume just the opposite. And that means the next depression will be deeper and longer than the last one.

In addition to the government's ability to prolong it, the tremendous burden of taxes and regulation will discourage the productive activity needed to rebuild. It will be more difficult to succeed in business.

And there are certainly far more liquidations to be made this time. The current inflationary cycle is probably the longest in modern history. So the price to be paid will be much greater.

The length of the cycle means that many glamour industries have developed, wholly within this cycle, and have created capital goods industries to support them. In some cases, an entire industry may be earmarked for liquidation. In others, only a fraction of the present firms within that industry could be sustained.

I would hate to be a producer of swimming pool accessories. Or worse yet, a producer of machine tools or other capital goods that are used solely in the production of swimming pools.

The electronics industry is probably shot through with products that are wholly inflation-created. And the space program may be exciting and breathtaking and wonderfully inspiring, but it's doubtful that our economic resources are at a level yet where they can realistically support such a program.

There are many, many exciting innovations that can be realities in our lives right now. But we're not willing to pay the price yet, *when we know what the price really is.* Those innovations *will* come; but only when technological achievements can make them available at realistic prices.

The next depression may mean the destruction of private credit.

Historically, it has been best to be a creditor in a depression and a debtor in an inflation. In an inflation, you want to borrow money and pay it back in cheaper dollars. In a deflation, you want to have money owed to you that will be paid back in more valuable dollars.

All well and good. But while you're sitting on your mortgages, you may find that the government will intervene to declare a suspension of debt repayments. You, as a creditor, will lose your source of income.

There will be no benefit to the economy from this; and it will probably destroy the incentive to ever again become a creditor.

Think of the next depression in terms of how things *may* be, not as they are now. See what has already happened and project it further along the same path. And don't think that any of the previous problems of depressions have been eliminated.

For example, don't assume that bank closings are a thing of the past. Banks are inherently insolvent—so long as they operate on the fractional reserve system. Bank runs could be triggered at any time. And the Federal Deposit Insurance Corporation doesn't have the reserves to cover even one good-sized bank failure.

I am *not* predicting bank closings or bank failures. But they are no less possible now than they were in 1929. If anything, they are more likely—because of the greater extent of inflation.

These considerations suggest the guidelines of a profitable course of action to follow. For it is an overlooked rule of success that *whenever others are beset with extreme difficulties, the man who has avoided these difficulties is in an unusually good position.* Here are some examples:

1. The government will undoubtedly increase its power in the next depression. Most businessmen will be entangled in a sea of red tape. Their operations will come to a virtual standstill; their businesses will be unprofitable and they won't even be able to liquidate them. They will not be free to act upon the opportunities that will exist.

Meanwhile, the man who has freed himself *before* the depression will have the pick of many opportunities. His capital will be liquid; he will have no entangling obligations and liabilities, no unsold inventories or commitments.

2. At the same time, most investors will have their assets tied up in unprofitable real estate holdings and other types of unsalable investments.

There will be many "golden opportunities" for investments, but few people will be able to take advantage of them. The man who has stayed away from the crowd, protected his capital, and kept it out of reach of confiscation, will be in a very fortunate position.

3. In the same way, if the banks *do* close, cash will be at a premium. Prices will drop to fractions of their former levels. The rare man who had the foresight to keep his money safe will be king. His cash will buy a great deal at that time.

To summarize, *liquidity* and *flexibility* are the keynotes. Recognize what *can* happen and be prepared for it. Not only will you save what you have, you'll be in a position to acquire much, much more than you had thought possible.

Most people will never think of these things. But now that you've thought about them, you're ahead of the game.

RUNAWAY INFLATION

Runaway inflation is undoubtedly the worst thing that can hit a highly industrialized nation. Once prices are changing daily, you know there is real trouble just ahead. Accounts of runaway inflation always dwell on the need to have a wheelbarrow full of paper money just to buy some groceries. But the most important consequence is the final destruction of the currency itself. Inevitably, the point is reached where the paper money is totally worthless. What happens then? There is no possibility of exchanging with paper money.

The government can issue a new currency. But unless it has gold reserves for backing (highly unlikely at that point), the new currency will be worthless. It will not be accepted by individuals who just lost all they had because of the last currency.

Historically, there have been only two ways that the economy could immediately begin rebuilding after having lost its currency. One way requires that "hard money" be available—gold or silver coins. If so, exchange can begin immediately.

But that usually isn't the case. Very rarely does runaway inflation take place in a nation where the citizens still have hard money. The private holdings of gold and silver provide a check on the government and prevent inflation from going too far.

Usually it is the second way that ends the standstill. That is for foreigners to come into the country, buy up property, and hire workers—using valuable foreign currency.

In the past century or so, the "foreigners" have almost always been American traders who came in with "good old Yankee dollars." The world has depended upon American entrepreneurial skill to keep things turning (long before foreign aid).

But what happens if it is America that has lost its currency? Where will the help come from?

There is little precedent to look to. There have been a few violent inflations in this country, such as the greenback era after the Civil War. But only certain kinds of currency suffered, such as the U. S. Notes which Lincoln dumped on the nation during the war. They became virtually useless in exchange. But there were still valuable gold and silver certificates in circulation, not to mention gold and silver themselves.

But what would happen now if our dollars became totally worthless? It's doubtful that foreign currency would have much acceptance here; we're not used to it as people of other nations are.

Our only salvation would probably be the silver coins that are currently hoarded in bureau drawers and basements. Let us hope the government does not succeed in melting them. For if it does, the one tool that could pull us through the crisis would be destroyed.

Even with the coins available, there would be a bad period before any order could be established. Once you begin to let your imagination run away with the possibilities inherent in hyper-inflation, the outlook can be pretty grim.

Without a currency, the government cannot operate its schools or police forces or pay tax collectors. Most likely, all governments in this country—federal, state and local—would collapse.

Your faithful "cop on the corner" wouldn't be there. He would be scrounging around like everyone else, looking for food to eat. Food supplies would no longer be coming into the cities.

Once all the grocery stores had been looted, the riots would become even more grotesque. The worst place in the world to be at a time like that would be in any metropolitan area. The old philosophy of home ownership that says "at least you'll always have a roof over your head" won't be attractive if the roof is 100 miles from where you'd consider it safe to be.

If you live in a metropolitan area, you certainly need to be prepared to get out in a hurry—to some pre-arranged area of retreat, far from any city. You need a place to go where there is food, protection, and shelter.

You can then wait out the worst of the crisis. When some semblance of order has been reestablished, you can return to civilization. If you have prepared yourself properly, you will have a large supply of silver or gold coins or both with which to acquire instruments of wealth.

If you live in a rural area now, be sure you're capable of being self-sufficient for a year or so. For if runaway inflation should hit the nation, you may not be able to count on the sources of supplies you're used to having.

The interim period sounds pretty distasteful, I know. But then, so does tuberculosis or war. And a look at the present economy indicates that the possibility of runaway inflation is far too great to be ignored.

But it only has to be grim if you are not prepared for it. If you are ready, you will not only be spared the worst; you will find an opportunity for new wealth.

This leaves one more possibility—a devaluation. Fortunately, this prospect is not so forbidding. In fact, it offers several opportunities to profit within the context of the present situation.

CHAPTER 12

If There's a Devaluation

$ $ $ $ $

"THIRTY-FIVE HUNDRED DOLLARS FOR A VOLKSWAGEN?! THAT'S AN outrage!"

Can you imagine being asked to pay $3,500 for a Volkswagen? That's stretching your imagination quite a bit, I realize. And yet that day may not be very far away. Not because of more inflation, which would drive up the prices of *all* cars; but, rather, because of a devaluation that would affect only certain foreign cars.

Such an event would certainly contradict the claims of commentators that a devaluation will have no effect upon your life. So let's look more closely at exactly what will happen if the dollar is devalued.

Fig. 3 helps us to place in proper perspective the various currencies of the world. Each government is acting as a warehouse for gold in its own country. It has issued money substitutes for the gold on deposit. Always, the money substitutes are given names like "dollars" or "francs" or whatever—to draw attention away from the amount of gold they are supposed to represent.[1]

---

1. This was brought to my attention in Murray Rothbard's booklet *What Has Government Done to Our Money?*

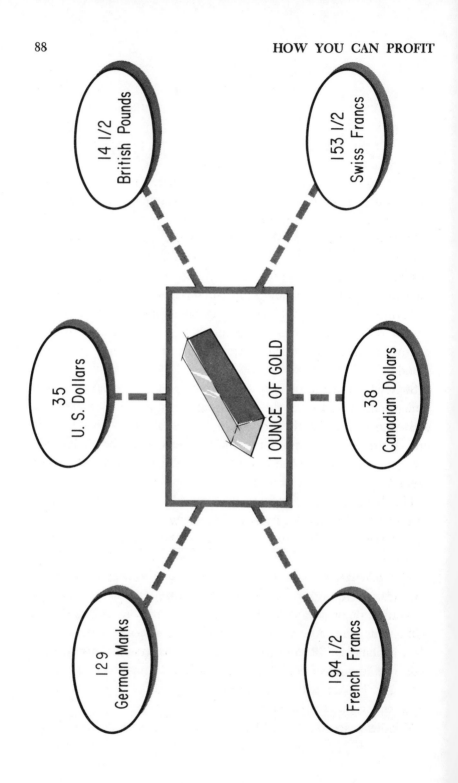

Even when the citizens of a given nation cannot exchange their paper money for gold (as in the United States), there's still a stated redemption ratio that applies to foreign governments and foreign central banks.

For example, the U.S. government agrees to redeem one ounce of gold for every 35 dollars turned in. The German government will redeem one ounce of gold for 129 marks; the French government redeems an ounce of gold for every 194½ francs turned into the French treasury, and so on.

If Americans are prohibited from owning gold, what do these redemption ratios have to do with our daily lives?

They affect us because of the paper money that is spent outside the country. Americans buy goods and services from importers who, in turn, pay in dollars to their overseas suppliers. Other dollars go out of the country as companies invest in overseas ventures, hoping to eventually bring back more dollars than they are spending.

Somewhere in the process, the dollars must be converted into a foreign currency. Either the American buyer or the overseas seller will eventually take the dollars to his bank, or to an exchange broker, to change them for a foreign currency. The dollars are not generally spendable in the foreign country; local currency is needed.

The bank, or the exchange broker, will change the American currency for the local currency. But on what basis? It will have to be based upon the amount of gold that each of those currencies is worth.

The gold ratios of the two currencies are compared; and a third ratio results: the ratio between the two currencies. Comparing the two ratios, one can calculate, for example, that 35 American dollars will redeem the same amount of gold (one ounce) as would 14½ British pounds. That means that $2.40 of American money would redeem the same amount of gold as would one British pound.

So the banker will make the exchange based upon the ratio: $2.40 equals one British pound.

Various ratios are quoted between various currencies (see Figure

4), all based upon the ultimate ratio to gold of each of the currencies. One dollar is worth about three and three-quarter German marks or five and one-half French francs or four and one-third Swiss francs or one and one-twelfth Canadian dollars, etc.—but only because of the ratio of each to gold.

THE PRESSURE BUILDS

When any government has inflated enough, too much paper money will have found its way overseas. That will create large pressures on its gold supply, even if its own subjects are prohibited from obtaining gold.

Finally, the pressure reaches a point similar to where our government is today. The gold stock is only a small part of what would be necessary to satisfy the claims of foreign governments alone.

Any moment a run on the gold, such as we had in March 1968, could break out. When that appears imminent, the government tries to protect the remaining gold by devaluing the dollar.

It announces that it will no longer redeem one ounce of gold for every 35 dollars turned in. Instead, for example, it will only redeem *one-half ounce* for 35 dollars; or one ounce for 70 dollars. It has made the dollar one-half as valuable in terms of the gold it will bring.

In effect, the government has reneged on its IOU's. It is paying off only 50¢ on the dollar—to use the jargon of the bankruptcy court.

How does this affect the prices of things? To find out, let's carry it a little further. We'll use the international silver market in London as our first example.

On a peaceful Friday afternoon, silver is selling in London for $2.00 per ounce. Well, actually it isn't. It's really selling for 200 pence—which is the British way of quoting the price.

At the official exchange rate, one British penny equals one American penny (it will vary slightly in the free market). So to obtain 200 pence, in order to buy an ounce of silver, an American has to put up $2.00.

Then comes Saturday morning. As you awaken to the news on

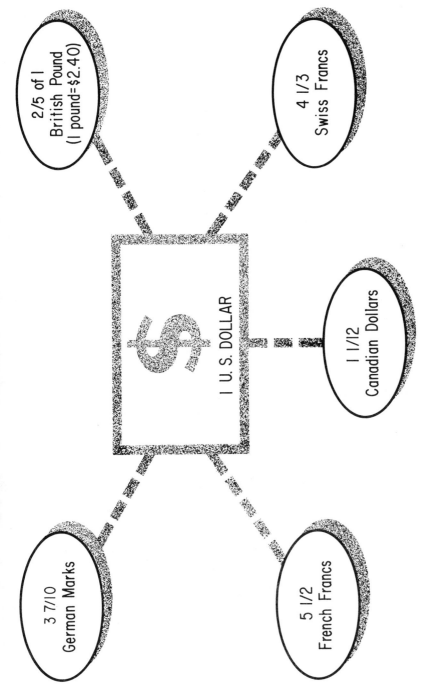

your clock radio, you hear that the American dollar has been devalued by 50%. Well, you've been told often enough that it doesn't concern *you*; so you roll over and go back to sleep.

On Monday morning, the London bullion dealers survey the market. They review their buy and sell orders, and they calculate that the day's price should remain unchanged from Friday at 200 pence.

But the price is not unchanged for an American. Because a dollar is no longer worth what it was on Friday. The bullion dealer can't exchange it for 100 pence any more, because the British bankers can no longer obtain 1/35 of an ounce of gold for every dollar they turn in to the U.S. Treasury.

At the new redemption rate announced by the American government, it would take $4.80 to equal the same gold value as one British pound. An English penny is now worth *two* American pennies. And 200 pence equals *four* American dollars, instead of two.

Over the weekend, the price of silver in American money has gone up from $2.00 per ounce to $4.00 per ounce.[2]

And this same phenomenon will exist wherever dollars are used to buy or sell in international markets. All international commodities will show an increase in price in dollars.

This is the effect of a devaluation. Now let's follow it further, to see how it affects various segments of the economy.

EXPORTS

An American exporter has various costs to pay to his suppliers in this country. The price foreigners are willing to pay for his products must be high enough for him to cover his costs and make an attractive profit, or else he cannot survive in business. So life for the exporter is a constant struggle to hold costs down and keep prices up.

But then the dollar is devalued. When it is, there is no change

2. This happened to the British when the pound was devalued in November 1967. The price of silver in dollars remained unchanged; but the price in pence went up 14%.

in his cost structure. Things in this country will still cost about the same (at least temporarily).

But a great change has taken place at the other end of his marketing line. Suppose his product sold for $2.40 in England. That would mean he was selling his product for one British pound.

If the dollar is devalued, it won't make much difference to the British people. What was worth one pound before will still be worth one pound. But one pound is now equal to $4.80 (assuming a 50% devaluation). That's twice what it was before in American money!

The exporter has suddenly received a windfall profit as a result of the devaluation. He will probably drop his price slightly, in order to stimulate more foreign demand; but his profit will still be larger than it was previously.

Soon enough, renewed inflation at home will start pushing his costs up. But his costs will have to *double* to be comparable to what they were before.

IMPORTS

The effect upon imports is exactly the opposite. With a 50% devaluation, they would double in price immediately, because of the change in currency ratios. The only exceptions would be imports from other nations that had just suffered a similar devaluation.[3]

Overseas suppliers, in countries where no devaluation had taken place, would require more dollars than they did before. They *could* lower their prices; but why should they? They can still get their old prices in other countries; it is only the American devaluation that has made their products seem more expensive here. However, if America is the chief market, then their sales will suffer and their prices will probably drop to some extent.

In any case, to the American citizen, the prices are much higher. The devaluation has not made him wealthier; nor has it given him

3. A few pages ahead, we will examine the likelihood of a widespread devaluation by several nations at once.

more paper money to play with. He simply faces higher import prices with the same old funds.

This, the politicians gladly proclaim, is the solution to the "balance of payments" problem (the outflow of dollars). Exports are stimulated and imports are discouraged. Of course, this means that we, as consumers, lose a great many attractive choices that were once available to us. And all to solve a problem that wouldn't have existed in the first place without the government's inflation.

The higher prices to Americans for imports will not result in more dollars being spent on imports. Rather, it will mean that fewer imports will be purchased. For the consumer doesn't have any additional paper money to spend.

It is important to realize that *resources are limited*. At any given moment in history, there are a fixed number of resources to be spent. Raising prices at that moment will only reduce the numbers and sizes of purchases.

This is a basic economic truth that is hard for many people to understand. Lack of understanding has created a widespread fallacy concerning the so-called wage-price spiral.

Resources are limited. So *price increases (without accompanying inflation) reduce the number of purchases that can be made.*

Only inflation can permit higher and higher prices. It is incorrect to think of labor unions, or anyone else, as causing inflation or higher prices by their wage demands. For where would the money come from to pay the higher wages? From higher prices? But where would the consumer suddenly get the money with which to pay the higher prices?

The fact that a union has succeeded in forcing a wage increase upon a company doesn't create the money with which to pay the increase. If the company attempts to pass the increase on to the consumer, it is just reducing the number of purchases the consumer can make with his limited resources.

Inflation feeds more paper money into circulation, which is then soaked up in many places and in many ways. And unions are part of the soaking-up process. But *without* inflation, customers could only pay higher prices by reducing *other* purchases. Unions would simply cause unemployment and business failures whenever they succeeded in forcing a wage increase. For there would be no extra money with which to pay the higher prices required.

How, then, would wages rise in a non-inflationary market? Through increases in productivity and increases in demand. Any time productivity increases reduce labor costs, most companies will share the added profit with employees, in order to hold on to the best of them.

Or if the company's services are in greater demand, consumers will be willing to offer more (at the expense of something else) in order to be first in line. Again, most companies will then bid higher to get better workers, in order to take full advantage of the ripe market. Companies that did not respond with higher bidding would lose the better workers to competitors.

But back again to the trail we were following. Price increases (without accompanying inflation) reduce the number of purchases that can be made. And this will apply to the higher prices asked for imports after a devaluation.

Demand will be lessened; for Americans would not have any greater resources with which to pay the higher prices. Even renewed inflation will probably not make up the difference.

Consequently, the price of silver, or any other international commodity, will go through a three-step process with regard to the price in dollars:

1. After the devaluation, the price in dollars would double (assuming a 50% devaluation), but remain the same in other currencies.

2. The higher dollar price would reduce American demand for the commodity. To whatever degree Americans were part of the market for that commodity, worldwide demand would be lessened.

3. This lessened demand would cause the price (in *all* currencies) to drop back slightly.

Using the silver example, we might then see the following sequence of events:

1. After the devaluation, the price jumps from $2.00 to $4.00; but remains unchanged for other currencies.

2. Americans buy less (and probably sell more) at the $4.00 price, causing a reduction in demand.

3. The lessened demand causes the price to decline a bit (in all currencies). The American equivalent might then drop from $4.00 to $3.50 or $3.75, for example.

EFFECTS AT HOME

At home, imports have become more expensive, but this doesn't mean that *no* imports will be bought. Even at higher prices, some will still be purchased.

In fact, some will have to be purchased if we are to continue to consume them. There are many products we rely on that aren't even made in this country.

If, after the devaluation, the total number of dollars spent for imports is the same as it was before the devaluation, it will have little effect upon American industries. We would then still have approximately the same number of dollars left to spend on these industries as we did before.

The distribution of purchases might change, however. For more money might be spent now on one industry (replacing an import that is now too expensive) at the expense of another American industry.

If, after the devaluation, the total amount of dollars spent for imports is *less* than it was before the devaluation, this should provide a temporary *stimulant* to American industry. For consumers would now have more paper dollars to spend on American companies. Again, the distribution pattern would be altered, to replace some of the foreign imports.

This is not to imply that we will be better off as a result. We will be worse off. We will be turning to second and third choices, after devaluation has priced the first choice out of the market. That's dandy for the second-choice seller; but it means a lowering of standards for the buyer.

If the total amount of dollars spent on imports is *more* after the devaluation (even though fewer imports will be purchased), it means that less can be spent on American companies.

In any of these cases, the result to the consumer is a simulated deflation. It is just as if he suddenly had less money to spend. He'll have the same number of dollars, but some prices will have gone up tremendously.

The net result of this will be as if a deflation had taken place. It will no longer be possible to buy as many things as were bought before. The standard of living will drop for American consumers.

Undoubtedly, most consumers will sharpen their buying habits to some extent, since they can no longer buy as much. Glamour industries will no longer be able to attract high prices. *The industries hit the hardest will be those that benefited most from inflation.* The stock market, land booms, luxury items, and other beneficiaries of inflation will be the first to suffer from the lack of spending money.

The highly touted "belt-tightening" procedure that is supposed to follow a devaluation is no myth. And it will induce consumers to confine their purchases to the most essential needs, thereby bringing on a readjustment period. And this in turn can send us straight into a depression.

The government will most likely turn on the inflation tap full blast at this point, official statements to the contrary notwithstanding. It is government's only hope for heading off a depression.

The devaluation will have brought temporary relief from the gold crisis; so the money managers will feel freer to inflate. Devaluation and deflation are two alternative responses to the gold drain. Devaluation permits immediate reinflation; deflation doesn't.

But one big danger of a devaluation is just that. The gold problem has been eased temporarily, but the danger of runaway inflation has not been lessened one whit by devaluation. Consequently, *the devaluation encourages the government to do the very thing (inflate) that will make runaway inflation more likely.*

The renewed inflation will send domestic prices upward again.

But quite a bit of inflation will be necessary before the deflationary effects of the devaluation will be overcome.

THE NET EFFECTS

Let's sum up the results of the devaluation.

1. Immediately following the devaluation, prices in dollars of all international commodities will be increased in proportion to the extent of the devaluation. Windfall profits will be made by those holding gold, silver, and other commodities in international markets, and by exporters.

2. The higher dollar prices will lessen American demand for many international products, causing sales and prices of those items to fall somewhat.

3. The standard of living in America will fall, due to the higher prices for imports. This will cause a readjustment period in which inflation-inspired items will be hit the hardest.

4. Although this is not an inherent component of the mechanics of devaluation, it is *very likely* that the government will resume inflation with relish.

5. This brings us right back to the depression–runaway inflation crossroads again. If the government does not get the inflation machine cranked up fast enough, the readjustment period (step three, above) may go too far and the depression will be on. But if it *does* manage to inflate fast enough, we'll be headed dangerously toward runaway inflation.

If, by this time, you're beginning to feel as if we live in a maze, where every apparent exit leads right back to the torture machine, *you're right!* The government, with its inflation, has put us in a hopeless position. It has long been too late for any "What would *you* do about it?" solutions.

At this point, all your thoughts should be directed toward what you can do to maximize your own position.

DEVALUATIONS IN OTHER COUNTRIES

What happens if another nation devalues and we don't? Not nearly as much, of course. We can summarize the basic effects upon various types of Americans, as follows:

1. Americans holding the foreign currency that has been devalued would be hurt, of course. It will exchange for far fewer dollars than they had counted on. This also applies to American businessmen operating in that country. If they have accounts receivable that are payable in the devalued currency, they will receive far less than they had contracted for.

2. Exports to the devalued nation will suffer—just as imports to this country would suffer from an American devaluation.

3. Imports from the devalued country would be cheaper to Americans (again, the reverse of an American devaluation). This would enlarge our alternatives, to whatever extent we rely upon imports from that country.

4. Demand for international commodities would drop, if any sizable share of the worldwide demand had been coming from the devalued nation. The higher price in the devalued currency will put the commodity out of reach of those buyers.

Holders of the devalued currency are the heaviest losers. These are primarily individuals or banks, not governments; so our government does not stand to lose too much from another government's devaluation. Consequently, our government has no true self-interest in trying to prevent a devaluation in another country.

In practice, however, our government takes an interest in everything and everybody; and it has done a great deal to try to keep the British pound afloat. At the same time, it apparently encouraged the French government to devalue in 1969.

WORLDWIDE DEVALUATION?

This leads us to a much discussed question: will most of the Western nations make an agreement to devalue their currencies all at once?

Many financial commentators believe this will happen. But why should it? What would be the point? How would it solve anyone's gold problem?

Why would the nations with strong currencies (such as West Germany or Switzerland) participate? A devaluation is a repudiation of one's debts. Why would a government that had done a relatively good job of maintaining the integrity of its currency suddenly declare bankruptcy?

Without West Germany or Switzerland, the participants in such a joint devaluation would be England, France, the United States, and a number of smaller nations that would be of no significance. We'd still experience all the major effects of devaluation already described. The dollar price of Volkswagens would still double, for example.

It is not impossible that the governments of these nations would *try* to solve their problems through a joint devaluation. They would probably liquidate all governmental holdings of foreign currencies (by mutual agreement) and then announce the joint devaluation. This would provide some relief to the governments, at the expense of individuals and banks that were holding devalued currencies. But the effects would be insignificant and temporary.

In no time at all, the gold drain would be just as critical. That means that, sooner or later, our government again would be forced to devalue—under pressure of losing all its gold.

The fiction of the Western governments standing together can only be maintained briefly. Solidarity simply means that the weaker governments help pull down the stronger ones (as Britain has been pulling us down for 30 years).

The luxury of solidarity will be cast aside when the chips are down; then it will be every government for itself. Two deadbeats can only exchange their checks so long, in an attempt to delude their creditors. Sooner or later, they have to come up with the real thing.

SEVERAL DEVALUATIONS?

Just as a joint devaluation might be attempted futilely, so a small devaluation might also be tried. The British did that with a 14% devaluation in 1967. With the U.S. government to bail them out, that devaluation has sufficed for an unusually long time.

But if the United States tries a small devaluation, there will be no one to lean on. This means another run on gold would be underway in short order; and that means another devaluation.

Sooner or later, the devaluation will have to be in the range of 50% to 67%, raising the redemption rate on gold to $70 or $105 per ounce.

WHEN?

There is no way to foretell the exact timing of a devaluation. It can come about as a cool, calculated political decision. Or a government can do it in desperation, under pressure from a run on its gold.

One point should be emphasized: don't pay any attention to statements by bureaucrats. They are totally meaningless. As former Defense Department official Arthur Sylvester pointed out, government officials feel justified in lying to preserve their own positions.

Henry Hazlitt, in his fine book *What You Should Know About Inflation*, has called attention to the classic example of bureaucratic fraudulence.

He cites a series of nine different statements made by Sir Stafford Cripps, then Chancellor of the Exchequer, denying that the British pound would be devalued.

These occurred between January 26, 1948, and September 6, 1949. They included such remarks as: "A reported plan to devalue the pound is complete nonsense"; "there will be no devaluation of the pound sterling"; "devaluation is neither advisable nor even possible"; "no one need fear devaluation of our currency in any circumstances"; etc.

Can you guess what happened on September 18, 1949?

Yes, the pound was devalued.

This is not an exceptional example. Money managers fear advance warning of a devaluation. They will deny it down to Friday night at midnight; and then devalue on Saturday morning.

And that's another point. Devaluations take place on weekends when the markets are closed. They come by surprise, whenever possible. So don't wait for a bill to be introduced in Congress before preparing for a devaluation. There won't be any bill.

The Cripps story is cited to warn you not to pay the slightest attention to any statements made by bureaucrats regarding the possibility of a devaluation. In fact, after the devaluation took place, Cripps defended his record of denials by saying, "No responsible minister could possibly have done otherwise than deny such intention."

Whether or not you agree with him, recognize that this is the way governments operate.

However, as already mentioned, the decision may not be made with cool, deliberate forethought. It may be forced on the government in the heat of a run on the gold.

In that case, you'll have some warning during the preceding week; but that's the worst time to hedge against a devaluation. The price of every hedge is shooting upward as other people are also trying to protect themselves.

If you buy your hedge then, you'll be paying a high price. And if the devaluation *doesn't* happen that weekend, the price of the hedge will drop again the following week.

So, by waiting until the last minute, you're putting yourself in a very difficult position.

Because its only alternative is deflation, *a devaluation is an overwhelming probability*. It's hard to believe that Richard Nixon would be willing to assume the Herbert Hoover image. It isn't that a devaluation will solve the inflation-caused problems; it's just that politicians generally *think* it will.

Since we live in an uncertain world, where *all* relevant factors can never be known, it would be foolish of me to make a prediction as to either *when* or even *if*.

Instead, let me say that I *expect* a devaluation to occur sometime between this coming Saturday and the end of 1971. I will be surprised (but not shocked) if it doesn't.

In the next chapter, we will take a brief look at business decisions, with respect to the possibilities we've been examining.

Then we will go into detail about devaluation's effect upon every major kind of investment. We will also see how each of these investments would be affected by runaway inflation, a short-term recession, a depression, or continued inflation.

It will be apparent that many popular hedges against these possibilities are *not* really hedges at all.

The Effects Upon Your Business

$ $ $ $ $

IT'S VERY EASY TO DEVELOP A "SPLIT PERSONALITY" ABOUT SOME things in life. You read a book like this, concern yourself with the investments you're making and how they will be affected by the possibilities we've been examining. Then you do something to make yourself less vulnerable.

And then, the next morning, you go back to your job at that multi-million-dollar swimming pool company.

But the world we live in is a single, complex entity. The events we're discussing will affect your investments, your business, even your purchases as a consumer.

Whether you own your own business or work for someone else, now is the time to take a good look at the industry in which you make your living.

The first question to ask is: How much has the industry been aided by inflation? Is the product or service involved a luxury that would not have fared as well if there had been no boom?

The industries aided most by inflation will suffer the most from a recession, depression, or devaluation. In many cases, companies will fail; in some cases, whole industries may be liquidated.

If you own or manage a business that's vulnerable in this way, wouldn't it be a good idea to make plans to get out of that business or to convert your operation to a less vulnerable line? Difficult as that might seem to be right now, it is much easier today than it will be next year or the year after.

If you are in a business that is not overly vulnerable, you will still have the basic problems of coping with the various phenomena we have seen. And you should begin today to make the necessary plans to be followed, if and when any of the possibilities occur.

Even in the present national economic conditions, there are certain characteristics of continued inflation that will affect you.

As this book has been saying over and over again, confusion reigns in an inflationary economy. It will become progressively harder to make accurate calculations of future business. The normal signals of consumer demand are distorted and will get much more distorted.

You naturally expect to be able to adjust to inflation, to take it into consideration in future decisions. But, somehow, more experience doesn't help any of us interpret trends in an inflationary economy.

One of the biggest business fallacies is the idea that large sales volume creates, or leads to, large profits. Inflation always leads you to believe that your prosperity is just around the corner. "Just a few more sales and we'll be in the black." But your costs will always be more than you expected. So the truth may be that the bigger your sales volume, the bigger your losses.

Traditionally, it has always been a virtue for an entrepreneur to think in the long term. The man who can engineer long-term plans will gain the greatest rewards in the market. But in an inflation, the very opposite is the case.

The longer the time span of your production or marketing plans, the more vulnerable you are to a host of unpleasant possibilities that didn't exist when you made the plan. Also, if inflation has caused you to miscalculate, you will have lost that much more before discovering the miscalculation.

So you should be looking for ways to deal more in the short term, with less dependence upon the far-off uncertain future.

This also means that you should arrange marketing programs and production plans with as much *flexibility* as possible. Put yourself in a position where you are not overly committed to a plan that could go sour because you had not calculated correctly.

If you haven't already done so, reread Chapters 10, 11, and 12 with your business or occupation in mind. Try to determine your vulnerabilities to each of the possibilities we've investigated. List them; and then set about eliminating as many as possible.

One way to eliminate vulnerability is to decentralize. Liquidate as much of your physical equipment as you can; then lease on relatively short-term contracts.

Wherever possible, eliminate employees from your payroll. Replace them by contracting for the services needed, either with individuals or businesses. In many cases, your former employee will be the new contractor. But your new arrangement will be far more flexible than the old one was; and it invariably will cost less.

Above all, recognize what we saw in Chapter 11—that the government has a bad habit of changing the rules in the middle of the game. Don't treat the present legal structure as a permanent condition. Laws change daily—inevitably toward greater governmental intervention.

Businessmen frequently lay out long-range plans that never reach fruition because they are thwarted by new government regulations. Always ask yourself, "What am I making myself vulnerable to? What kinds of new regulations could hurt me?"

Arrange everything with a maximum flexibility in mind. Don't put yourself out on a limb where the bureaucracy will saw you off.

The government is a fact of life; and it will become a larger and larger consideration in your business as time passes. But if you stay flexible and alert to loopholes, you can minimize its interference and continue to profit.

Of course, there is the alternative of thinking that you personally will be able to change the government's mind and change the course of history.

But, to me, that would be the most foolish course of action.

CHAPTER 14

Standard Inflation Hedges

$ $ $ $ $

WE'RE READY NOW TO TURN OUR ATTENTION TO SPECIFIC INVEST-
ments. In this and the next two chapters, we will look closely at
each of the major types of investments: stocks, bonds, real estate,
etc. It's doubtful that any kind of investment has been overlooked.
Investments made directly in businesses were covered in the last
chapter.

Since there are a large number of investments to look at (18
types), they have been loosely organized into three major categories: (1) those that are normally considered to be hedges against
inflation; (2) those that are normally considered to be hedges
against recession or depression; and (3) a group of "independents"
that revolve more around gold and silver. One chapter is devoted
to each of these categories.

Each investment will be checked against each of the five basic
possibilities we've been following: continued inflation, recession,
depression, runaway inflation, and devaluation.

Where an investment group looks good, you will still have
to exercise selectivity within that group, to decide specifically where
to place your funds. There is no attempt made in this book to
recommend specific stocks, etc. Even when a group looks bad,

some specific investments in that group may go against the trend.

Obviously, your greatest interest will be in looking at those investments you already have or are contemplating at this time. But if you take the time to read all of the three chapters, it should help to reinforce what we've already seen—especially since this will be the practical application of the theoretical ground we've covered.

STOCKS AND MUTUAL FUNDS

Mutual funds are dependent upon stock market movements, so they are being included here. We are interested in seeing how stocks in general would perform in any of the possible conditions.[1]

The stock market is a prime beneficiary of inflation. Miscalculating their resources, many people believe they have extra funds with which to invest, when they really do not. This initiates an upward push in stock prices, drawing other funds from fixed-return investments that do not keep up with inflationary cost-of-living increases.

Continued Inflation: So stocks are not only an inflation hedge; they run ahead of increases in the general price level. As long as the present cycle continues, the stock market is a nice place to visit.

Recession: In any kind of deflation, stock prices drop faster than the general price level drops (the reverse of inflation). The readjustment atmosphere hits the stock market first, even if there is no drop in the general price level. Each recession will be brief, however. It will either respond quickly to reinflation or it will be transformed into a depression.

Depression: When the general price level starts moving downward in earnest, stocks will really tumble. And if you then have to sell at the bottom, the price will not be a reflection of the new, lower general price level. Your sale proceeds will not have as much purchasing power as you gave up to buy the stock in the first place.

1. Gold and silver stocks will be considered separately in Chapter 16.

You will hear the old cliché that many mutual fund companies and "blue chip" stocks survived the depression and paid dividends right through it. But that is of little comfort. Your resources will be tied up for years waiting for those companies to regain their former prices.

Runaway Inflation: Even though the stock market is a nice hedge against normal inflation, the picture changes drastically when runaway inflation hits. When the currency breaks down, it will put companies out of operation. Who can trade or pay employees without a currency? And there are questions of vulnerability to riots and looting.

Your stock certificates would be worthless under those circumstances. If the company did somehow live through the crisis, there is no guarantee that your property right would be respected in the new order of things. And how would the stock exchange operate without a currency?

Devaluation: Because it is an inflation-oriented investment, the stock market will suffer in the simulated deflationary conditions following a devaluation. There may be some individual stocks that will gain because the prices of their foreign competitors will have become prohibitive. But the market as a whole should drop much more than most people expect.

There may, however, be a brief period, immediately following the devaluation, when prices will be bid upward. This will be the result of the prevailing ignorance about such things. The market should ultimately drop quite far.

Comments: If you want to be in the stock market, selectivity is important. Prices don't move *en masse*; they fluctuate individually.

But the stock market is no longer a very attractive place for a cautious investor. It is only profitable as long as the present cycle holds; and we have already seen the difficulties encountered in sustaining it during 1969.

Since the blow can come at any time, you'll have to have nerves of steel to stay in the stock market now. With what is coming at us like a tidal wave, don't you find it difficult to visualize yourself standing on the beach, waiting for the very last moment before running?

Under the circumstances, *the "blue chip" stock market is for gamblers only today.*

COMMODITIES

This group concerns farm commodities, metals, etc. traded mostly in the futures' markets in Chicago and New York.[2]

The only favorable climate for commodity investment is the present inflationary cycle; and, even there, it is terribly risky. This book was not written for the individual who is a full-time speculator, but for the man who is a part-time investor. And the commodity markets are no place for the part-time investor.

In an interview published in the Los Angeles *Times*, Robert J. O'Brien, chairman of the Chicago Mercantile Exchange, referred to a Department of Agriculture survey that indicated that only 25% of all grain speculators made a profit in 1967. He also said that only 2% of all commodity contracts actually reached delivery date. That means 98% of the action comes from speculators; only 2% from actual participants, users, or producers of the commodity.[3] In short, it's a market for professional speculators.

Continued Inflation: If you happen to be a full-time professional, then the market should remain generally bullish as long as the present cycle lasts. Naturally, selectivity is highly important here; specific market conditions of various commodities prevent the overall market from moving in any kind of unified fashion.

Recession or Depression: In either case, commodities will suffer. Since so much of the action is speculative, a great deal of paper money will be drained out of the commodity markets during a deflationary period.

Runaway Inflation: The same problem exists here as with the stock market. The commodities markets would undoubtedly close because of an inability to exchange without currency.

2. Silver bullion will be treated separately in Chapter 16.
3. Los Angeles *Times*, November 13, 1968.

Devaluation: Only metals that are traded largely in international markets are likely to profit from a devaluation. Other commodities will probably suffer in much the same way that stocks will. Even if you use silver futures, or some other metal as a hedge against devaluation, your timing has to be very good, if you use margin. On an all-cash basis, or the equivalent, you would not have that to worry about; but there are better ways to hedge against a devaluation.

Comments: There is really nothing to commend the commodities market to the part-time investor. Even if there were, it would be highly vulnerable to governmental intervention. The silver market in New York was closed from 1934 to 1963 as a result of governmental taxing interference. The same thing could happen again.

INCOME REAL ESTATE

This group includes any kind of real estate aimed at drawing income: apartments, rental houses, commercial office buildings, industrial property.

During any inflationary boom, income property always looks attractive. But *overbuilding* is typical in any inflation; and the consequences are rough when the boom is over. There are individual exceptions to this, of course; a medical building is not quite as vulnerable as a popular-priced resort. But there are other things less vulnerable than medical buildings, too.

Better and better office buildings, more luxurious apartments, frills of all kinds. These are common in inflation. But they are often unrealistic.

Continued Inflation: If you own income property now, this would be a good time to get rid of it. That doesn't mean the price might not be a little higher next year. But the price might also be a great deal *lower* next year; and that is a worse risk.

Current conditions may be all right in general for income property, but it's going to get harder and harder to make rational decisions. Prices and demand signals will begin to get more confusing.

Recession: The extent of the damage done to you during a recession will depend largely upon what kind of tenants you have. If you have tenants who are not going to be driven out of business by a brief interruption of the inflation, you may weather it all right.

Depression: But here you will have problems that are much worse. The lowering of the general price level will necessitate lower rents in order to keep tenants. And what if you have a high mortgage on the property? The financing leverage you thought was so attractive can destroy you in a deflation.

This is when the overbuilding shows up. Undoubtedly, there will be many empty buildings. You'll have no liquidity unless you're willing to sell at a much lower price than that at which you bought. And that may not be possible if you have a mortgage.

If creditors are legally allowed to repossess mortgaged property during the depression, there may be an excellent opportunity to purchase property. Homes in relatively well-protected areas would be recommended, since business conditions would remain very uncertain.

Runaway Inflation: This will be a totally untenable situation. There will be no liquidity in your investment. You will be liable to riots and looting. Tenants will have no currency with which to pay their rents. If you feel you have to stay where you are, be sure you obtain tenants who have saved plenty of silver coins.

Devaluation: With the deflationary conditions involved, money will be drawn away from frills. The time lag between devaluation and sufficient inflation may be too long for you to weather. It will depend mainly upon the kind of tenants you have, as is the case with a recession (covered above).

Comments: The only value here is in continued inflation. But even there, it requires perceptive market decisions during a state of confusion. So if it can only be "possibly good" during only the short term, then why get involved?

RESIDENTIAL REAL ESTATE

This section refers only to ownership of your own home.

Additional property that is rented to others is covered under *Income Real Estate*, above.

There are two possible reasons why someone would purchase a home. The first is because he desires the control of his own property that home ownership provides. That we can refer to as the *enjoyment value*.

The second reason is because he believes that it is a *profitable investment*. While that *can* be true in some instances, most of the superficial financial benefits turn out to be illusory on closer examination.

You buy a home for $25,000 and sell it a few years later at $35,000, and there seems to be a $10,000 profit. But inflation has caused other prices to go up, and a good part of your apparent profit is just the general price level increase.

In addition, it is easy to overlook the sums of money you have paid out—taxes, repairs, interest, capital improvements, and the like—things a renter doesn't have to be concerned with. And what about all the wages you should have paid yourself for the labor expended on upkeep?

When all these things are taken into consideration, it is quite likely that your return after selling your home (less broker's commission) will be less in real dollars than what you paid for it. On the other hand, you will have saved a good deal of rent.

When you put the two together, any profit you have left is *entrepreneurial profit*. That is what you receive for having picked the right house in the right area; in other words, a correct marketing decision. This is the same profit the landlord makes—but only when he happens to be right.

These remarks are made not to discourage home ownership; but only to discourage the idea that home ownership is a consistently good financial investment. In the cases where it turns out to be all of that, it is only because of a good marketing decision—the kind you would have to make in any other type of investment in order to profit.

If you're going to buy a home, do it realistically; recognize that you are doing it for the *enjoyment value* that comes from controlling your own property.

Continued Inflation: It does not appear that the residential real estate market is a special beneficiary of inflation; it probably about breaks even with inflation.

If you do not feel the area in which you now live will be comfortable during an economic crisis, now should be the time to sell. It may be that there will not be another period in which it will be fairly easy to sell.

Recession or Depression: Since the premise here is that home ownership should not be approached as a financial investment, the only relevant consideration is how immobile it makes you. It will be very difficult to liquidate during a depression. You may then have a mortgage much bigger than the market value of your home.

If you're intending to keep your present house for the next ten years, and you have a small mortgage or none at all on it, and you're out of the metropolitan areas, then a depression probably won't affect you badly.

But don't overlook the alternative of renting instead and having a pile of cash with which to approach the depression.

As mentioned earlier, it's possible that the government will intervene to bestow "relief" on mortgage payers, at the expense of their creditors. But I would not want to be in the position of counting on either side of that possibility.

Runaway Inflation: If your home is in a metropolitan area, you can only describe the specter of runaway inflation as highly dangerous. You won't be able to sell your home for anything worthwhile; possibly, you'll wind up trading it for something that normally has little value.

You will be vulnerable to chaos and looting. Under those conditions, home ownership will not necessarily be synonymous with "having a roof over your head." We've already seen a great deal of painful and costly rioting in America during the past few years. It shouldn't be too hard to visualize the consequences of runaway inflation.

Devaluation: There will be the same general conditions following a devaluation that accompany a recession. Liquidity will be impaired, but real estate values should not be reduced for too long.

Comments: Here is a suggestion, a sort of double hedge. Sell your home and find a home of comparable quality to rent. Obtain as short a lease as possible. If you had no mortgage on your home, you probably won't like the idea of having to make monthly payments; so deduct five years' rent from the proceeds of the sale; and put it in a savings account of the kind that will be recommended in Chapter 18. If you had a mortgage, there's no special reason to have your rent payments set aside in advance.

Use the rest of the capital from the proceeds to invest in some of the more conservative aspects of the investment program to be recommended in Chapter 18.

If after five years none of what has been projected in this book has come to pass, withdraw your capital from the investment program and buy a home again. Most likely your capital will have appreciated more in the investment program than it would have in your home, possibly enough more to cover the rent payments.

But, most important, this plan will give you flexibility, opportunity, and peace of mind during a time of great uncertainty. With a large investment tied up in your home, you just may have trouble sleeping at night. But with your capital totally liquid, you'll be ready to take advantage of any situation that may develop.

When you recognize that home ownership is primarily an enjoyment value, not an investment, you'll probably find that you can rent just about any kind of home you might want.

But if you're determined to own your own home, consider finding an area less vulnerable to some of the chaos that may be ahead.

LAND

"Land booms" are almost always inflation-inspired. The only exceptions are land sales resulting from the discovery of oil or some other permanently valuable resource—a sudden reason, unexpected but realistic, for developing a new area.

This is not to say that raw land is not a realistic investment. It can be. But a great deal of the subdividing being done today would have no market without inflation.

In Southern California, for example, residents are bombarded with offers from literally scores of different developers—mostly of desert property. Some of that property may demonstrate a durable value; but most of it is appreciating purely from an inflationary demand.

Land, for most people, can be called an investment frill. It appeals quite largely to income groups that do not do a great deal of investing. But with proper financing and occasional inflationary rises, it has a great attraction as a way to becoming an investor.

In general, land that has been purchased as part of a large subdivision is the most likely to be an inflation-inspired investment. So it is the most vulnerable to economic crisis.

Continued Inflation: The primary benefit of the *status quo* would appear to be the time it provides for liquidating land investments. Already, individuals are finding it difficult to sell parcels of land purchased in many of the Southern California desert developments. But whatever the proceeds, they most likely will be more valuable if used elsewhere.

Recession or Depression: Even land in metropolitan areas will have little liquidity during a deflationary period. There is usually very little building during such periods, so land is not in very great demand. However, if the area looks safe enough to you, it may be profitable to build on your land during a time of extremely low construction prices (if unions and government allow building costs to drop during the deflation).

Runaway Inflation: At least if it's raw land, there's nothing to loot. But you'd have to hold it for the long, long term in order to get anything worthwhile for it. And, in the meantime, you might have trouble protecting your ownership of it.

If the land is in the right place, it might be suitable for a retreat. Put an A-frame on it, stock it with the bare necessities, and have your own resort for vacations—or a retreat, if chaos comes. But don't approach this as a *capital gain.*

Devaluation: There will be many people trying to sell their land parcels during a post-devaluation period. If you're prepared to wait out that period, the devaluation will probably not affect you one way or the other.

DIAMONDS, JEWELRY, AND ART OBJECTS

For people who like something a little more exotic than the stock market, a good hedge against inflation has always been found among diamonds, jewelry, art objects, antiques, and rare coins.

Continued Inflation: These objects are prime beneficiaries of an inflationary cycle, for the same reasons given for other investment frills. But they are primarily the province of professionals who know what they're buying.

Recession: Prices will suffer during a recession, even though the general price level may not dip. But it should be a fairly short-term period.

Depression: What was a benefit during inflation will be a bad liability during a depression. Prices will nosedive. Even at low market prices, you may have trouble finding a buyer. These investments can be valuable only if you are prepared to hang on for a long, long time. But why not have your assets in something else of value during the interim, then buy back the art objects later, when they can be purchased for a fraction of their former costs?

Runaway Inflation: Although these were ideal inflation hedges, they are useless for a runaway inflation. You cannot liquidate them, with no currency available. You could barter them only for very large purchases, but only if you could find a prospect. Otherwise, you couldn't spend them. How do you make change for a 3-carat diamond?

Devaluation: Diamonds that are sold freely in international markets can be a source of profit from a devaluation. They will appreciate in dollars from the change in currency rates. Manufactured jewelry and art objects may not be as valuable, unless they can be easily sold in foreign markets soon after the devaluation.

Since such investments are not usually handled on margin, your profit may not be as great as it might be with precious metals.

Comment: Despite the glamourous nature of these investments, they are mostly inflation hedges. And it is time to start switching to depression hedges and runaway inflation hedges.

CHAPTER 15

Standard Depression Hedges

$ $ $ $ $

DURING AN INFLATIONARY PERIOD, DEPRESSION HEDGES NEVER appear very attractive. But Andrew Carnegie claimed that one of the cornerstones of his success was his ability to develop a strong cash position during inflationary times. He then used it to buy up facilities and capital goods during deflationary periods.

That philosophy is still sound today. However, the government is making each succeeding depression a little stickier than the previous one; and there are pitfalls to be avoided, which we will recognize as we proceed.

CASH AND SAVINGS ACCOUNTS

Carnegie probably didn't show much return on his cash position while he was accumulating it during inflationary periods. But his object wasn't the interest rate at that point. It was liquidity for the times he knew were coming.

Continued Inflation: The latest credit squeeze in 1969 is evidence that savings accounts cannot keep up with inflation. The only justification for a savings account is its liquidity. But that can be more than enough—provided you're sure the cash will be available in all circumstances.

Recession: Cash isn't as good as it might normally seem. As mentioned before, there will probably be very little drop in the general price level, if any. There will be liquidations, but possibly not of the things you would want to buy.

Depression: But here cash comes into its own. Then the lower price level would make it possible to acquire some potentially good investments. However, the normal value of cash for consumer goods might be neutralized by minimum price levels enforced by the government. It's less likely that capital goods and investments would be price-supported.

Runaway Inflation: As others have said, if runaway inflation hits, I hope your home is decorated in green; because your cash will be useful only as wallpaper. Once you see prices moving every day or two, get rid of whatever cash you have as fast as possible.

Devaluation: Despite the simulated deflation, prices will probably not drop much; so your cash will not be of any special value. There will be some business liquidations; but probably not anything you'd want to acquire.

Once there is a devaluation, you should be especially alert to the possibility of runaway inflation following.

Comment: Since bank holidays can never be legislated out of existence, be careful about normal savings accounts. Despite the loss of interest, keeping cash in a safety deposit box in a *non-banking* institution will allow you to sleep more easily.

BONDS AND TREASURY BILLS

Included in this group are bonds of governmental agencies, corporate bonds, and U.S. Treasury bills.

Continued Inflation: The interest paid on the bonds is comparable to what you are losing through inflation. So you're just breaking even.

Recession: The value would remain somewhat stable, and you would continue to draw the interest.

Depression: This is the one eventuality for which bonds are attractive. The redemption value will remain stable while the general price level is falling. As a result, this is a traditional hedge against depression.

But there is always the threat that if times get hard enough (and they might), the government can default on its promise to pay off the bonds.

Wouldn't they do that? What is a devaluation, if not a defaulting on a debt?

Runaway Inflation: Treasury bills and bonds are liquid in any other situation; but in runaway inflation, they will be totally worthless.

Devaluation: All things considered, bonds would not be affected much—one way or the other.

Comment: Bonds are only of advantage if you are sure we are headed straight for a depression. Even then your timing must be pretty good; for bonds fluctuate in price after they are issued. If you can buy them when they are underpriced, they can be better than cash. Convertible bonds have additional alternatives, but you pay for them in a higher price; and even these alternatives don't cover all the possibilities we're concerned with here.

MORTGAGES AND OTHER LOANS

Traditionally, it's better to be a debtor during inflation and a creditor during deflation. There are the pictures of the "penny-pinching" bankers who get rich in a depression by foreclosing mortgages. Factually, the picture leaves a lot to be desired, however.

The banker does not show much profit during a depression. He has not been lending his own money. Rather, he has been borrowing at one interest rate and lending at a higher interest rate. The difference is his profit.

When an economic crisis hits, those who have claims against him exercise those claims. Depositors want their money. But his capital is tied up in long-term loans that cannot really be called in unless the borrower defaults.

If the borrower should default, the home can be repossessed.

But the recovered asset is usually worth less than the mortgage at that point. Sure, the banker has acquired some homes—but it will be years before they will be worth anything.

This same principle applies, whether it is a bank, savings and loan, mortgage company, or any other form of lending agency.

In addition, governments traditionally intervene on the side of the debtors during hard times. As far back as the depression of 1819, state governments passed various laws to prevent creditors from receiving payments due them.

Continued Inflation: There is obvious erosion of your investment in an inflationary cycle. When you are repaid, the dollars you receive will buy less than those you originally lent. Purchasing trust deeds at a discount helps to compensate for this, but they are not bargains. The discount is merely a recognition of the depreciating value and the high risk involved in such a transaction. And the interest runs a race with the rising general price level.

Recession: Probably the only time when an individual can actually repossess property advantageously is during a recession. The short-term readjustment period can cause a borrower to default; and the depressed real estate market will probably rebound with the next bout of inflation. But if your timing is bad, and it is really the advent of a depression, you will have white elephants on your hands.

Depression: If you foreclose on a $15,000 mortgage and repossess a house that's worth only $12,000 in the current market, how have you gained? You would have been much better off to have held onto your original $15,000.

Your only hope is that your borrowers continue to make their payments. If they *do*, what you receive will have appreciated in value, thanks to the deflation. But it is a highly uncertain business.

Runaway Inflation: Obviously, this works to your disadvantage. The borrower can pay you off in cheap dollars any time he chooses.

Devaluation: The simulated deflation will create similar circumstances to that created by a recession.

Comment: There is too much uncertainty connected with any of the possibilities to make this an attractive investment.

LIFE INSURANCE AND RETIREMENT PLANS

This concerns life insurance as an investment. That means whole life policies, annuities, endowments, retirement plans, pension programs, etc.

In cash-value insurance policies, the premium includes two components: what you are paying for the life insurance itself and what you are paying into a savings account that is drawing interest.

This is not a discussion of the value of life insurance itself; we are viewing only the savings account part. To determine how much is involved, subtract the cost of a comparable term insurance policy from the premium of your cash value policy.

Continued Inflation: As long as the interest earned on your cash value savings can keep up with inflationary increases in the general price level, you are breaking even. But we may be past that point already; in which case you may actually be losing money.

Recession: Here you have a relatively stable value plus interest.

Depression: The traditional value is the increased buying power of a fixed amount of dollars while prices are falling. Most insurance companies should survive a depression, just as they did before. But there has to be a point at which their investments in inflation-inspired land holdings can destroy them.

Runaway Inflation: Your policy would be worthless; because there would be no currency with which the insurance company could pay you.

Devaluation: Theoretically, you shouldn't be affected one way or the other. But we've already seen that a devaluation will encourage the trend toward runaway inflation. And since life insurance policies are usually undertaken for the long term, it will require some will power to get out of the policy when it becomes evident that you should.

Comment: The only value is for deflationary possibilities. Even in continued inflation, you are beginning to lose.

It would make sense to convert to term insurance. Determine the amount of protection you would want your beneficiary to have; then add 50% for inflation. There is no reason to add more than 50%; for beyond that, the economy will be headed toward making your policy worthless.

Most companies will not allow you to convert your cash value policy to term insurance without taking out a new policy (physical examination, etc.). So it would be wise to make the change now, rather than wait until some time in the future when you may be less able to qualify. In closing out your cash value policy, you will be paid the accumulated value of your policy to that date.

SELLING SHORT

"In 1929, I sold short." In the popular song, those words describe the man who does everything right. Anyone who sold short before the crash probably made a fortune. The word "probably" is appropriate, however; because there are factors of stock selection, timing, etc.

Obviously, the time to sell short is just before a deflation. Since news of credit restrictions always brings a speculative sell-off in the market, you lose a good deal by waiting for such obvious timing indicators. However, if you know what you are going to do in advance, and then execute it immediately upon hearing such news, you will probably reap most of the benefit.

The individual stocks to select would be those with the most "air" in their prices, usually those with the highest price-earnings ratios. In other words, the stocks that have been helped most by inflation will probably drop the fastest in a deflation.

Continued Inflation: Not the time for this, of course.

Recession: Useful perhaps as a period in which to test your ability to pick the right stocks for short selling.

Depression: This is the best time. Somewhere along the way, as the stocks start dropping, an "air pocket" is hit where there are *no* buyers and the price drop is straight down.

Runaway Inflation: No.

Devaluation: This may be a real sleeper. As we have seen, there will be a simulated deflation after the devaluation (dependent upon the amount of dollars still spent on imports). There are many opinions expressed about the effects of a devaluation; but few people recognize the deflationary possibilities.

Prices in general will not fall; but stock prices, in general, will. With a good selection of stocks, a short seller might do surprisingly well at this time.

In addition, the readjustment period caused by the devaluation could plunge the economy into a depression. If that happens, the timing will have proven to be ideal.

If you decide to do this, pick your stocks now. Choose the prime beneficiaries from inflation, those most likely to plummet in the deflationary post-devaluation period.

Once the devaluation happens, watch the stocks continually from a broker's office. The stocks will probably continue to climb for awhile. But when one drops 5% from its post-devaluation high, sell short (or place a *put*). That should be your best timing. If it then rises 10%, cover your *short* and take your loss.

Comment: Short selling is a glamourous idea, and there *will* be some fortunes made that way. But it really isn't appropriate for a part-time investor. It will require full-time attention, careful selection, good timing, and an iron constitution. It is a go-for-broke idea—recommended for bachelors only.

If you *do* get involved, consider using *puts* (options to sell) rather than selling outright. It's a hedge against your own mistakes. It will reduce your potential profit, but the insurance is worth it.

CHAPTER 16

"Real Money" Hedges

$ $ $ $ $

THE TIME WHEN YOU MOST NEED REAL MONEY (GOLD AND SILVER) is when it is generally respected the least.

When governments are abandoning gold and silver, when commentators are saying that we can get along without them, when people don't seem to care one way or the other—that is the time when you'd better turn your assets into gold and silver.

For that is the time when the most unrealistic monetary ventures will be undertaken. Currencies will fall; savings will be destroyed. The future will be rebuilt by those who were smart enough to ignore the mass psychology.

Real money means gold and silver. But that isn't the end of it. As we saw in the second chapter, the man who produces the money commodity has no inside track to wealth. There are inefficient gold miners, just as there are inefficient druggists.

In this chapter we will survey three investments based upon gold, three based upon silver, and one that is somewhat related. Some of these investments look better than others; and even the favored ones require further selectivity.

SILVER BULLION

Some have asked whether silver coins will disappear. The answer is very definitely—No. Our present coins won't disappear and they won't even become rarities . . . If anybody has any idea of hoarding our silver coins, let me say this. Treasury has a lot of silver on hand, and it can be, and it will be used to keep the price of silver in line with its value in our present silver coin. There will be no profit in holding them out of circulation for the value of their silver content.

President Lyndon B. Johnson, July 23, 1965[1]

The President was saying, in effect, that the price of silver would not go over $1.29 per ounce, the monetary price of silver. His confidence was based upon a hoard of silver that the U.S. Treasury had accumulated over a 90-year period. As long as the U.S. government was willing to sell silver to anyone in the world at $1.29 per troy ounce, there was no way the price could go higher.[2]

But contrary to many such governmental forecasts, on May 17, 1967, the Treasury announced it no longer had enough silver to continue selling worldwide at $1.29. It limited its sales to privileged American industrial buyers. The price *did* move upward; and the silver coins *did* stay hidden.

In terms of yearly production versus yearly consumption, the world had been short of silver for several years. As long as the Treasury hoard could make up the difference, there was no apparent shortage. But once the government curtailed its sales, the shortage became critical.

For the next year, the price rose fairly steadily, reaching a high of $2.55 in May 1968. Then the Treasury loosened its grip on the remaining reserves and more silver flowed into the market, sending the price downward. By October 1968 it was back in the $1.80

1. At the signing of the new coinage act—quoted in the Annual Report of the Director of the Mint, 1965.
2. Gold and silver are always weighed in terms of *troy* ounces, rather than avoirdupois ounces. All references to ounces in this book are troy ounces.

range; and, with slight fluctuations up and down, it remained in that range through 1969.

During 1968, the Treasury accumulated around 200 million ounces of silver coins, which it then melted and sold to industrial silver users. By leveling off the weekly sales at two million ounces, it managed to keep the market in balance.

The Treasury predicted that it would continue doing this for several more years (just as it had earlier predicted it could hold the price at $1.29 into the 1970s); but there was nowhere near enough silver in the till to back that up.

In the spring of 1969, the government lifted its ban on the private melting of silver coins, apparently to prepare the way for its own withdrawal from the market. Possibly by the time you read this, the U.S. government will be completely out of the market.

If this happens, the price will probably be over $2.00 per ounce again. And it will still have a long way to go upward.

Silver is in far shorter supply throughout the world than the government has been willing to admit. Rising prices will not stimulate production—for two reasons: (1) silver is not widely available to be produced; and (2) 80% of the silver produced comes as a by-product of the production of lead, zinc, copper, or gold. Why would a copper miner, who derives maybe 10% of his revenue from silver, increase his production—just because the price of silver is rising?

On the other side of the market, industrial consumers have found no acceptable replacements for any of the more important uses of silver; and it is very unlikely that they will do so in the next few years. Consequently, their demand for silver will not be reduced much by higher prices.[3]

It would not be surprising to see the price of silver in the $4.00 to $6.00 range by the end of 1971 (augmented by whatever inflation does to the general price level).

Continued Inflation: As the above information indicates, the

3. The economics of the silver situation are summarized in Rickenbacker: *Wooden Nickels,* and Smith: *The Economics of Silver.*

price of silver bullion should appreciate over the next two to three years, based purely upon market considerations.

Recession: It will be affected by any brief readjustment period, when speculation will inevitably be pinched—for the same reasons that stocks will. But since silver and gold are havens of safety in uncertain times, silver would probably not suffer drops of the magnitude that most stocks would.

Depression: It is very possible that silver prices might benefit from a depression. Industrial use will drop, but probably not as much as production—since the latter is so dependent upon copper, lead, and zinc production, traditional losers in a depression. This could *increase* the shortage.

At the same time, however, the general price level will be dropping, including that of silver prices. Again, silver and gold are havens in times of uncertainty. So it is difficult to say how all these factors will combine to affect the silver price in a depression. If there's a drop, it should not be very great.

Runaway Inflation: Silver would weather a hyper-inflation. It is even liquid during a crisis, if you take your proceeds in a foreign currency that is alive.

Devaluation: As we saw earlier, the price of silver will appreciate in dollars in proportion to any unilateral dollar devaluation. Silver is an attractive devaluation hedge. Since you can buy bullion on margin, you can use a portion of your assets to protect all of them.

Comments: Silver bullion is one of the best all-round investments, especially for what we will probably be facing in the next few years. You will be protected against any possible disasters. In fact, you will *profit*—whatever direction the economy might take, including a continuation of the *status quo.*[4]

It is well within the realm of possibility that the U.S. government could one day confiscate silver, as it did gold. Certainly the government has shown that much interest in silver in the past. Since you don't *have* to take a chance, keep your bullion outside of the United States.

4. Jerome F. Smith first called my attention to several of the above considerations.

Silver bullion should be bought for present delivery. Stay out of the futures' market, for all the reasons indicated in the section on commodities in Chapter 14.

With the exception of gold, there is no particular attraction in any other precious metal (platinum, palladium, etc.).

GOLD BULLION

American citizens and other residents of the U. S. are legally prohibited from owning gold bullion, here or anywhere else in the world. Since it is possible that this book may be read by individuals outside the United States, we will examine gold bullion as we have other investments.

Just as the U.S. government kept the price of silver down to $1.29 for many years, so it held down the price of gold. The government made it a policy to sell as much gold in the free market as was necessary to keep the price from rising above $35.00 per ounce (which is, automatically, the official gold price in any other currency also). Whenever the demand for gold threatened to push the price upward, our government unloaded some of its reserves—to meet the demand and prevent a price increase.

Finally, in 1968, a full-scale run on gold threatened to wipe out the American gold supply. A hasty solution was adopted: governments would settle international trade balances by trading gold with each other at the official redemption rates ($35.00 and its equivalent in other currencies); but there would be no more attempt to hold down the free market price with governmental gold reserves.

The governments of the Western nations pledged *not* to sell any of their gold reserves in the free market (to take advantage of the higher prices there). Suddenly there was a really free market in gold, since our government was no longer dumping its reserves there to hold down the price. In no time at all, the price passed $40.00 per ounce.

Continued Inflation: Gold is real money; and that's what people turn to, if they can, when inflation runs rampant. Citizens of France, West Germany, and a few other countries buy gold when their own governments get out of line. In addition, since so much seems to depend upon the United States, continued inflation here adds to the worldwide demand for gold.

The free market price is not necessarily going to go straight up, however. In late 1969, it dropped back to $35.00 per ounce when chances of an early dollar or pound devaluation temporarily lessened. There will be many such fluctuations—but the overall trend will be upward.

Recession: The gold market is a worldwide market; so a U. S. recession would probably not affect gold bullion adversely. If anything, it could encourage foreign investors to get into gold, until the uncertainty ends.

Depression: If the depression is worldwide, prices of most everything will fall. Gold prices will be supported somewhat by the flight to gold in crisis times. On balance, gold should profit; but it is not certain.

Runaway Inflation: Gold is an ideal asset during a runaway inflation, provided the gold is stored in a safe place. It is liquid if you take your proceeds in a currency that is not suffering from the crisis.

Devaluation: A doubling of the redemption rate for dollars will double the dollar price for gold in the free market: so gold bullion is a prime beneficiary of devaluation.

Comments: There is good reason for non-U.S. citizens to include some gold bullion in their investment programs. But it is not worth the risk for an American citizen to violate the law. The investment program recommended in Chapter 18 will cover everything that owning gold bullion would have done for him.

Since gold is not a scarce commodity, in the way that silver is, it does not have the same supply-and-demand pressure to push the price upward. And any of the monetary factors that will send gold upward should eventually affect silver anyway.

Because gold and silver are particularly important, and because gold and silver stocks are likely to move contrary to the general market, these stocks are treated individually here, instead of being included in Chapter 14.

GOLD STOCKS

Here again, as with other investment groups, selectivity is important. In fact, *especially* here—since there is definite value in holding gold stocks. Much further investigation will be necessary to find the individual companies whose stocks represent the best buys. The mere fact that a firm mines gold does not mean it is efficient, durable, or that its stock is a bargain at present prices.

Once you have found the gold stocks that are priced right and are durable, the following considerations apply:

Continued Inflation: Gold stocks should continue to appreciate in the present economic climate. We now have a free market in gold; the gold price should seek its own level and then continue to appreciate as currencies depreciate further.

There will be intense monetary speculation in gold—causing some wide fluctuations, as currencies look dim, then revive.

All of these factors will invariably affect the prices of gold stocks. But the ultimate attraction of gold stocks will be the inevitable devaluation and, possibly, the eventual worldwide adjustment of gold prices.

In the meantime, some South African stocks are paying dividends of 6–10%. So these stocks are unusually attractive, even without a devaluation.

Recession: Since there has been a true free market in gold only since 1968, there is little precedent by which one can predict the reactions of gold stocks to various phenomena. If you own South African gold stocks, and the recession is in the United States, the effect *should* be upward pressure on the prices. This would come as a result of the uncertainty generated by the U.S. recession, with little of the deflationary effects upon the South African price levels (except as U.S. citizens provide a market for those stocks).

Depression: Here the lack of a precedent creates a mystery. With deflation affecting speculation on the one hand, and the flight to gold from uncertainty on the other, we seem to have a toss-up. However, the precedents that *do* exist demonstrate that gold stocks run counter to prevailing trends. The gold price is constant while costs drop. The stock of Homestake Mining had a low in inflationary 1928 of $40. Its high during 1937 (the depth of the depression) was $1,080.

Runaway Inflation: Gold stocks will survive hyper-inflation, provided the companies involved are not in the nation suffering the runaway inflation. There may not be absolute liquidity during the crisis. But after the run is over, the demand for gold should be even greater—as a result of the graphic example of the crisis.

If you hold stock in a company in the nation suffering runaway inflation, sell it at the first danger signal.

Devaluation: With a change in U.S. redemption rates to $70 or $105 (or anything else), the free market price of gold does *not* automatically change. Neither does the price of gold change in any other currency. It will be only the *dollar price* that changes.

Consequently, the dollar price of gold bullion will increase and the price paid in dollars to American gold mining companies will go up. *But it will not necessarily affect any companies in nations where devaluation has not occurred.*

In South Africa, the gold mining companies sell their output to the government, which, in turn, markets the gold to the world. Those companies can only profit from a devaluation if the South African government changes its *own* redemption rate. And the South African government has very little incentive to do that.

If the U.S. government devalues to a $70 per ounce basis, it will double the number of dollars South Africa will get for each ounce of gold sold to the United States. That means a doubling of the goods it can buy from the United States, without increasing its own output in any way. South Africa's chief export is gold; the small harm done to other South African exports will be incidental, compared to the gain realized on gold trading.

It appears to be official policy for the South African government to pass on any such benefits to the gold companies. But the only sure way those companies can benefit is by higher free market demand for the bullion itself—not by changes in redemption rates, which do nothing more than change currency ratios.

Because currencies are receipts for gold, visualizing the effects of devaluations on the various prices for gold can be a tricky business. I must admit that, for a long time, I assumed that South African gold companies would automatically profit from a dollar devaluation.

But for the reasons just outlined, the South African *companies* are the poorest bets—if you're counting on a devaluation for their ultimate profits. As a group, their stocks are holding up well in price, in anticipation of a devaluation; but only because most speculators are incapable of visualizing the effects of a devaluation.

It should be recognized, however, that the stocks may even skyrocket in a mistaken post-devaluation hysteria. But eventually those prices would have to collapse.

In chapter 12, we saw the three-step post-devaluation process by which silver (for example) would increase its dollar price, then slip back in all currencies. This is because the higher dollar price reduces buying pressure from the United States.

The same thing will be true of gold. Higher dollar prices for gold will be reflected in the free market—as far as Americans are concerned. This will discourage American demand. Also, there should be an especially large sell-off by those who've anticipated the devaluation correctly. These two factors would apply downward pressure on the free market price.

The ultimate result *could* be a dollar price for gold in the market that would be *less* than the U.S. government's new redemption rate. That would take *all* the pressure off the government's gold supply for awhile. (And it would really encourage further inflation.)

Summarizing the preceding data, it is recommended that American gold stocks be bought to assure full profit from a dollar devaluation. And South African stocks should be bought because their prices will probably go sky-high from purely emotional and unrealistic reactions right after the devaluation.

When that happens, watch all of your stocks continually during trading hours. *Sell a stock automatically when it has dropped 5% from its post-devaluation high.*

In so doing, you *may* miss its final high. But chances are you'll come very close. And the higher post-devaluation profits from American gold mining companies will make them extremely vulnerable to government intervention. That's another reason I'd rather be out as early as possible.

There is one more fallacy that should be dealt with. You might call it the "multiple earnings" fallacy. It goes like this: Ajax Gold Mining Company (a fictional company) sells gold in the free market at approximately $40 per ounce. At this price, it makes $3 per ounce net profit and pays a pretty fair dividend. If the price of gold goes to $70 per ounce, it will not change the company's costs at all. So its profit per ounce will jump from $3 to $33, an elevenfold increase. If the price of gold doubles, the stock will more than double; it will go up about 11 times.

The fallacy is in thinking that the company's costs will not go up. As we saw above, that is not the case. Higher prices mean higher costs—not the reverse, as is commonly thought. The company whose profits are going up will begin to bid higher for workers and equipment in the market, hoping to produce more and get a larger share of the higher-priced market.

And in this case, it will be bidding primarily against its own competitors—*who have the same extra bidding power*. This will neutralize part of the added profits.

This does not mean that earnings will *not* go up. They definitely will. But don't get carried away and expect them to go up in a geometric progression.

Many investors *will* be waiting for those higher dividends, however; and they may temporarily bid the stock unrealistically high.

Comments: Even though the American gold stocks are more likely to gain, they are *not* an unmixed blessing. The American companies are subject to governmental pressures, regulation, and even the possibility of nationalization.

In buying gold stocks, recognize the risks you are taking and be moderate in your investment. Buy both American and South African stocks for diversification. Even if one group loses, the gains of the other group should more than offset that.

SILVER STOCKS

In general, silver stocks should parallel changes in the price of silver bullion. Most of what was said regarding silver bullion applies here. But, just as with gold stocks, there will be differences in performance between various companies.

Continued Inflation: Silver-producing companies should profit from the supply-and-demand factors that were reviewed above.

Recession: Silver stocks would probably decline in a brief recession, along with most other stocks.

Depression: As mentioned earlier, the price of silver will probably go up after the depression has been underway for several months. This should increase the value of those companies that produce silver exclusively.

Runaway Inflation: The stock can only be useful if the company survives intact; and it isn't likely to survive a runaway inflation. In addition, the stock exchanges would be closed.

Devaluation: If the dollar price of silver goes up, American companies will profit from the devaluation. But beware of the "multiple earnings" fallacy that was detailed above.

Comments: Only an American company would profit from a dollar devaluation. And American companies are too vulnerable to regulation and possible nationalization.

In addition, the price-earnings ratios are generally very high on those stocks that are already producing silver. Those companies that aren't yet in production will have to wait a very long time before showing profits and dividends.

There is nothing a silver stock can do that silver bullion cannot do; and silver bullion lacks some of the vulnerabilities of the stocks. So the bullion looks much more attractive.

SILVER COINS

There are two distinct markets for silver coins. Although it is not generally recognized, they are entirely different markets.

As we have seen, most of the silver coins disappeared from circulation during 1964–1965, because of inflation. Two years later, the price of silver finally sprung loose from $1.29 per ounce. As a result, silver—in all forms—was suddenly in greater demand.

Thus silver coins have a value in two ways: (1) they can be melted down, the silver content refined, and sold on the market as *bullion*; and (2) they are *silver coins* with all the values of a true coin (recognizable weight and fineness). Once melted, the silver no longer has its value as a coin, but begins to take on value as bullion.[5]

In either case, it is the silver content that makes the coin valuable. But this expresses itself in two ways: as a *coin* (a "real money" medium of exchange) and as *potential bullion*.

Continued Inflation: In the current economy, the coins profit from both markets. They will rise in value on the coat tails of silver bullion; and, as coins, they will become more valuable as inflation becomes even more pronounced.

Recession: There may be a slight drop in value during a brief recession.

Depression: As coins, silver hasn't the strength that pure cash would have. Cash is always acquired at face value. The face value will buy more as prices drop.

But you cannot acquire silver coins today at face value (except for a stray dime or quarter given to you in change here or there); in early 1970, you paid the face value plus about 40%. So the general price level has to drop that 40% first, before any further price drop can increase the buying power of the face value of the coins.

However, the bullion potential of the coins may go up, for the reasons mentioned before.

Runaway Inflation: For this possibility, silver coins are an absolute necessity. They will be the only spendable money around.

5. We are referring here to what is called "junk silver"—silver coins that have *no* numismatic value. Coins of specific, valuable dates are treated under "Diamonds, Jewelry, and Art Objects."

Particularly useful will be the dimes and quarters—as opposed to half-dollars or silver dollars. The lower units give you more liquidity.

Devaluation: The bullion potential will profit, for the reasons we have already reviewed. The coinage value will become more critical, too, because of the likelihood that stepped-up inflation will follow.

Comments: Buy silver coins as the ultimate hedge against runaway inflation. There are dealers who sell the coins in $1,000 bags and finance them. The bags are stored in a bank. That is a different kind of investment, and it may be used in place of silver bullion. We will discuss it further in chapter 19. Here we are concerned with silver coins as the ultimate form of spending money.

Keep the coins at home. Think of them as a form of absolute security, not as a traditional profit-making investment.

GOLD COINS

It is illegal for American citizens and other residents of the United States to own gold bullion. But it is *not* illegal, at this time, to own gold coins of any nation, *provided they are dated 1933 or earlier* (because they are considered collectors' items).

This is a way for Americans to own gold. However, you pay a premium price, mainly because the gold is more valuable in the form of coins.

Continued Inflation: With a free market in gold, they should continue a basic long-term trend upward.

Recession: Again, we have the problem of a lack of precedents, because there was no true free market in gold prior to 1968. But you could expect the dollar price to drop somewhat in an American recession.

Depression: If gold becomes more popular as the result of a long-range economic crisis, that might tend to neutralize a downward trend. But, basically, the price should drop in a depression.

Runaway Inflation: Gold coins would be far less useful than silver coins as spending money, because of their higher value per unit. But once you have stored enough silver coins, you can use gold coins for large purchases of property, capital goods, businesses, or anything else. The holder of a large supply of gold coins may be in a position to create a new fortune after the chaos is over and rebuilding has begun.

Devaluation: The coins are bound to reflect the higher bullion prices. They can be an excellent replacement for the individual who is legally prevented from owning gold bullion.

Comments: American coins are preferable to foreign coins— because the gold content will be more easily recognizable. However, some foreign coins have the weight of the gold content stamped on them.

SWISS FRANCS AND OTHER FOREIGN CURRENCIES

This type of investment is included in this chapter because it serves the same basic purpose as gold and silver.

The only currency to be recommended is the Swiss franc. Other currencies run hot and cold. The German mark was highly popular in 1969; but no more so than the French franc had been a year or two before. And the French franc certainly has gone sour in the interim.

Strangely, the Swiss franc does not have the stable value it is often thought to possess. Heavy shipments of money into Switzerland create inflationary conditions, causing volatile changes in the currency exchange rates. Switzerland is a small country, so foreign investors can cause imbalances in the Swiss economy.

Yet, through it all, the Swiss franc is a safe currency, backed up solidly by gold. Whereas the American dollar is really only 4% backed by gold, the Swiss franc is 82% backed by gold. With that much difference, it is apparent that the statement "If the dollar is devalued, all the other currencies will be, too" is not very realistic. Why should the Swiss devalue such a sound currency?

There is a vast difference between the currencies. Compare these figures with those on page 67.

SWISS FRANC PAPER MONEY SUPPLY
(converted for comparison into dollar equivalents)
(October 1968)

Current Account Deposits:	$ 720.7 million
Currency in Circulation:	$2,489.6 million
Total Money Substitutes:	$3,210.3 million
Monetary Gold Stock:	$2,648.3 million

(Source: Swiss National Bank)

Continued Inflation: By keeping the Swiss francs in a Swiss bank, you will earn between 4½ and 5% interest. That is about what you can get in a savings account here, but hardly an attractive rate. But if the American inflation speeds up, a 5% rate on Swiss francs will actually be larger when converted back to dollars. So you do not need to fear any greater inflationary loss of value. The main reason for such an account is to maintain liquidity.

Recession: Since we're not expecting much of a change in the purchasing value of the dollar during a short-term recession, you will neither win nor lose by having the Swiss francs.

Depression: Here you would lose some purchasing power, since the dollar would certainly gain in value. But you would have greater security and liquidity in the Swiss franc; and that means greater peace of mind—which should make the loss worthwhile. The chances of a Swiss bank failing are not nearly as great as those of an American bank.

Runaway Inflation: The Swiss franc would certainly preserve your store of value; but during the few days of the actual runaway period, there would be no liquidity. You wouldn't want to convert any francs back into dollars because they'd immediately lose their value.

But as soon as the run was over and any new medium of exchange developed, the francs would be liquid—whereas many other types of investments we've seen would not be.

This would give you resources with which to acquire articles of wealth, once some stability had been restored to the community.

Devaluation: It *is* possible (although not probable) that the

Swiss franc will be devalued eventually. But it certainly will not be devalued in the absence of a dollar devaluation; nor will it suffer a larger devaluation. If there is a simultaneous readjustment of currency ratios, the Swiss franc will probably have the smallest devaluation.

If the dollar is devalued, and not the Swiss franc, you may want to protect yourself by quickly converting your Swiss francs back into dollars. There is always the chance of a Swiss franc devaluation *following* the dollar devaluation.

Since there is little chance of two dollar devaluations in quick succession, you have everything to gain and nothing to lose.

Comment: The principal value of Swiss francs is in their cash liquidity and their invulnerability to both U.S. banks and U.S. dollar devaluation.

CHAPTER 17

The Balance Sheet

$ $ $ $ $

WE'VE COVERED A LOT OF GROUND SINCE WE EMBARKED ON PAGE one to have a look at the nature of the monetary crisis.

To be sure we haven't skipped anything important, let's summarize the principal characteristics of each of the possibilities, and see which investments respond in the best way to each of the possibilities.

CONTINUED INFLATION

There is no way to foretell how much longer the present inflationary cycle can continue. But we do know that the longer it lasts, the more hectic it will be. There will be more frequent "quickie" recessions, followed by renewed inflation.

This means more confusion, more difficulty making rational business, financial, and personal economic decisions. A farsighted individual will use this period to get his house in order, eliminate his vulnerabilities, and create the framework by which he can profit from the coming events.

Here are the 18 investments, classified by the ways that continued inflation will affect them:

Very good: Diamonds, art objects, etc.; stocks and mutual funds.

Good: Cash (for liquidity), commodities (but risky for the amateur), gold bullion, gold coins, gold stocks, income real estate, undeveloped land, silver bullion, silver coins, silver stocks.

Break-even: Bonds, life insurance, mortgages, residential real estate, Swiss francs.

Bad: Short selling.

RECESSION

The absence of a drop in the general price level is the most significant feature of contemporary short-term recessions. At the same time, however, there will be considerable drops in the prices and liquidity of inflation-inspired items.

Good: Gold stocks, short selling.

Break-even: Bonds, cash, gold bullion, life insurance, mortgages, Swiss francs.

Bad: Commodities, diamonds, art objects, etc., gold coins, income real estate, undeveloped land, residential real estate, silver bullion, silver coins, silver stocks, other stocks, and mutual funds.

DEPRESSION

All indications are that the next depression will be more severe than the last one was. The politicians have managed to make the current inflationary cycle last longer than any previous one.

Therefore, the liquidation period will be even more difficult than the 1929 readjustment. And greater governmental interference will make the next depression much more prolonged. You should be prepared for everything that happened before—and for things that may be much worse.

This means that some of the investments indicated below as attractive may also be vulnerable to government intervention.

Very good: Bonds, cash (outside of banks), short selling.

Good: Gold stocks, life insurance, silver bullion, silver coins, silver stocks.

Break-even: Swiss francs (safety).

Uncertain: Gold bullion, gold coins.

Bad: Mortgages.

Very bad: Commodities, diamonds, art objects, income real estate, undeveloped land, residential real estate, stocks, and mutual funds.

RUNAWAY INFLATION

This is the worst possible thing that can happen. If it hits, you want to be as far as possible from metropolitan areas. You want to be well stocked with what you need to survive, including silver coins for trading purposes.

Very good: Gold bullion, gold coins, gold stocks (not in the country where runaway inflation occurs), silver coins.

Good: Silver bullion, silver stocks (see gold stocks, above), Swiss francs.

Very bad: Commodities, diamonds, art objects, income real estate, land, mortgages, residential real estate (in cities), short selling, stocks, and mutual funds.

Worthless: Bonds, cash, life insurance.

DEVALUATION

If after the devaluation the number of dollars spent for imports is as big or bigger than it was previously, a deflation-like atmosphere will set in. There would appear to be better than a 50% probability that this will happen.

Exports will flourish until renewed inflation at home cuts into profits. Imports will be hurt.

Any asset you hold in an international market, where the price is measured in dollars, will give you a profit from devaluation. Immediately after the devaluation, you can convert back to more dollars than you originally spent for the asset. But some assets will profit far more than others.

Expect inflation to be renewed with vigor after the devaluation.

Very good: Gold bullion, gold coins, gold stocks, short selling, silver bullion, silver coins, silver stocks, Swiss francs.

Good: Diamonds, art objects, etc.

Break-even: Bonds, cash, life insurance, mortgages, residential real estate.

Bad: Commodities, income real estate, land, stocks, and mutual funds.

On page 146 you will find a summary of all the investments we have examined.

The quick review in this chapter was intended as a summary of the material we have already covered. Do not act upon any of these recommendations without consulting the more detailed explanations given in previous chapters.

Now we are ready to put all of this together into an investment program that will enable you to profit, no matter which way the economy goes.

SUMMARY

Investment	Inflation	Recession	Depression	Runaway Inflation	Devaluation	Comments
Bonds	Break-even	Break-even	Very good	Worthless	Break-even	Timing required
Cash, savings accounts	Liquid	Break-even	Very good	Worthless	Break-even	Banks vulnerable
Commodities	Risky	Bad	Very bad	Very bad	Bad	For professionals only
Diamonds, etc.	Very good	Bad	Very bad	Not liquid	Good	Professionals' market
Gold bullion	Good	Break-even	Uncertain	Very good	Very good	Illegal for U.S. citizens
Gold coins	Good	Bad	Uncertain	Very good	Very good	American coins
Gold stocks	Good	Good	Good	Very good	Very good	Sell after devaluation
Life insurance[1]	Break-even	Break-even	Good	Worthless	Break-even	Term insurance only
Mortgages	Break-even	Break-even	Bad	Very bad	Break-even	Too risky
Real estate, income	Good	Bad	Very bad	Very bad	Bad	Time to sell
Real estate, land	Good	Bad	Very bad	Not liquid	Bad	Inflation-inspired
Real estate, residential	Break-even	Bad	Very bad	Dangerous	Break-even	Rent for flexibility
Short selling	Bad	Good	Very good	Very bad	Very good	For bachelors only
Silver bullion	Good	Bad	Good	Good	Very good	Don't buy futures
Silver coins	Good	Bad	Good	Very good	Very good	Cash basis only
Silver stocks	Good	Bad	Good	Outside the U. S.	Very good	Bullion safer
Stocks, mutual funds	Very good	Bad	Very bad	Very bad	Bad	More risky every day
Swiss francs	Break-even	Break-even	Safe	Good	Very good	No other currencies

1. Includes retirement plans.

CHAPTER 18

The Investment Program

$ $ $ $ $

WE LIVE IN AN UNCERTAIN WORLD. NO ONE CAN HOPE TO GATHER all the information necessary to predict with certainty the timing of specific events.

But this doesn't stop us from seeing the broad picture of what is to come. We know that certain acts produce certain consequences. Since those acts have already taken place, it is now just a matter of time until the consequences come.

As I wrote this book, the thought kept nagging at me: "I hope it doesn't reach the market too late!" And yet, it may prove to have been published two years earlier than necessary. If so, it is far better to be ready two years too early, rather than *one day* too late.

It has been mentioned already that *there are no precedents* to guide us in certain areas. There has never been, for example, an all-out runaway inflation in this nation. As a result, we can only use logic to project the conditions that would prevail.

There are similar historical vacancies about technical reactions of gold stocks, free market bullion prices, etc., to a devaluation.

The scientific method is a four-step process: (1) *observe* the world around you; (2) *draw conclusions* concerning cause-and-effect relationships; (3) *make tests* to see if you can accurately predict results; and (4) *refine your principles* through continued observations and tests.

Where we have no precedents to guide us, we are limited to the first two steps. There is no way we can *test* our conclusions until the one all-important moment comes.

We can only observe the world around us, draw conclusions, and make decisions based upon the principles we have created. Then we must wait for the crisis to see whether or not our logic is airtight.

I make no claims to omniscience or infallibility. The uncertainty of the situation prompts me to recommend a diversified program for you. My attitude is the same with regard to my own investments.

That doesn't mean we're operating in the dark, though. Far from it. Compared to the prevailing economic thought, we are working under the brightest light of understanding. Clichés, like those examined on page 68, seem to be the answers to all serious problems these days. The politicians of the world are working with band-aids to patch over the problems until their successors take office.

Compared to the multitudes, you and I will fare extremely well —because we have been willing to trust our own minds, rather than trust the politicians.

THE PROGRAM

What is required is an investment plan that will give you *good* growth (not necessarily *maximum* growth) in assets as long as the present cycle lasts; plus protection, liquidity, flexibility, and buying power in the next depression; safety and rebuilding power in the event of a runaway inflation; an excellent profit from the devaluation; and the ability to sleep nights in the interim.

The program consists of six investments. First, they will be summarized. Then we will look at each of them in detail.

1. *Cash in dollars:* Have enough cash on hand (actual currency, greenbacks) to pay your bills for one month under normal

circumstances. If you want absolute safety, do not keep it in a bank. Either store it at home or in a safe deposit box that is *not* located in a bank or savings and loan company.

Use your checking account to pay current bills only. Leave money in your account only long enough to write checks to pay your bills. Do *not* keep a savings account in a bank or savings and loan company.

2. *Swiss francs:* Send your savings to a Swiss bank; and convert them to Swiss francs. *This* is your savings account. The Swiss bank, if properly selected, will be invulnerable to the problems that an American bank might face in a depression. You will have buying power—even if everyone else finds his assets frozen.

3. *Silver coins:* Have $250, or more, in silver coins. Keep them at home or in another safe place outside of a bank. This is your absolute safety in case runaway inflation strikes. Their value will appreciate, even in the absence of such a crisis. But their main value lies in their universal purchasing power.

4. *Silver bullion:* Invest in silver bullion for its growth possibilities, as well as to capitalize on the devaluation. Buy through a Swiss bank; that way you're not vulnerable to a possible nationalization, or confiscation, of silver in this country.

5. *Gold stocks:* These will give you a further profit from the devaluation, capital growth as long as the present cycle continues, and further diversified protection against a depression.

6. *Retreat:* Also important, for peace of mind, is the creation of a retreat—some place where you can go if matters reach their worst. It should be far away from any metropolitan areas. Even rural areas will only be safe if the local residents are largely self-sufficient and individualistic. This part of the program includes anything you might do to give you protection, mobility, and freedom from the chaos and rioting that would accompany runaway inflation.

RESULTS

In the next chapter, we will go into each of these investments in more detail, outlining the mechanics of executing the program.

But first, let us review each of the possibilities to see how our investment program would be affected:

Continued Inflation: The cash will provide no profit, but will give you safety; it is, in effect, an insurance policy. In the same way, the Swiss franc savings account will not provide a profit (the interest on the account will permit you to break even with inflation). It will provide important liquidity for any possibility to come.

The bulk of your investment capital will be in profit-making areas, however. The silver bullion should appreciate steadily and the gold stocks, if selected carefully, should profit from the rising free-market price of gold.

The silver coins will increase in price along with the silver bullion, so you will be showing a profit there.

The retreat will not show a profit. But if you select it to be an attractive vacation spot, it will pay its way regardless. Make it as comfortable a hideaway as possible; so that you will enjoy being there during good times.

Your total capital should increase fairly substantially within 18 months from the implementation of this program.

Short-term recession: This is the only possibility in which you will show a loss; but there are very few good investments for a recession. We have intentionally sacrificed this possibility because it will be very short-lived. Whichever way the economy goes from there, you will be covered well.

In the event of a recession, you will break even on the cash and the Swiss francs. The gold stocks may appreciate, but your silver bullion and coins will probably depreciate slightly. The retreat will not be affected one way or the other; it will simply not be necessary yet.

Depression: If a full-scale depression hits, the cash will continue to be valuable because of its safety from bank runs. The Swiss franc savings account will provide the liquid funds with which to buy, at bargain prices, the things that will comprise the foundation of your new future.

The silver bullion and coins should profit, for reasons covered in Chapter 16. Gold stocks will most likely appreciate greatly. The retreat will probably not be necessary under these circumstances; so it will be on the books as a loss.

Your investments will probably experience considerable growth in value during the depression. In addition, you will have the cash with which to buy many other things that will grow in value as things begin to return to normal.

Runaway Inflation: If this happens, the silver coins will enable you to survive the runaway period, and to trade with others afterward. You should be at your retreat; the city will be no place in which to live at a time like this.

When you see retail prices starting to move every other day or so, spend your cash for anything you need (just get rid of it usefully). Dispose of any American gold stocks you're holding (and possibly your South African stocks, too); convert the proceeds into silver coins and head for your retreat. You'll pay a big premium for the coins at that point, but they'll be more valuable than worthless paper.

Leave the Swiss francs and the silver bullion in your Swiss account. They'll be worth a great deal to you when the crisis is over. In the meantime, your retreat should be well stocked so that, with the silver coins, you can last a year if you have to.

Devaluation: When the devaluation happens, you will score very well. Your gold stocks may be worth several times their former value. As indicated before, sell them at the first post-devaluation peak—unless it appears that the devaluation was too small and another will follow.

The silver bullion will at least double its value (given a 50% devaluation). If you use leverage, your profits will be even bigger. You may want to take your profits immediately after the devaluation, waiting to see which way the price of silver will go then. The coins will have been purchased on a cash basis, so they will profit to the extent of the devaluation.

The Swiss francs will also profit to the extent of the devaluation. After it's over, convert them back to dollars—just in case the Swiss franc should be devalued in the aftermath.

While these four assets will be increasing in value, prices will remain relatively stable here for the near term. You may want to bring some of your profits home and spend them while you can still do so.

The retreat will not be affected by the devaluation; neither will the small amount of cash you're holding.

SUMMARY

The only eventuality that will not provide a profit for you will be the short-term recession, and it should be just that—short-term. As long as you have some liquidity, there is nothing to do but simply wait it out.

In the event of a depression, some of your investments will show a profit, and the Swiss francs will give you buying power at the most opportune time. And in a runaway inflation, you'll not only have precious safety, but assets that will be appreciating and providing the basis for new wealth in the aftermath.

A devaluation will compound your capital several times over on one Saturday morning. And even if nothing happens, a continuation of the *status quo* will permit good profits for you in silver and gold.

CHAPTER 19

How to Do It

$ $ $ $ $

YOU ARE AN INDIVIDUAL HUMAN BEING.

As such, you are a different human being from me.

Those two statements are self-evident. And yet, it is very easy to overlook the differences that exist between individuals. Each person has his own nature, his own interests, his own objectives, his own fears, and his own ideas (among many other distinctions).

If you were to ask me to tell you specifically what you should do about the problems discussed in this book, I could only answer that question after a long and detailed study of *you*. There are so many individual matters that must be taken into consideration; there is no way one person can provide the answers for everyone else.

How much protection should you have? That depends upon you. It depends upon such factors as your age, your marital status, the number of your children, any other dependents, and your future earning power. And it also depends upon such psychological factors as your willingness to gamble, your patience, and your capacity to tolerate unpleasant circumstances.

There is no way that this book could possibly take such individual matters into consideration. Rather, the book is designed to show you the possibilities that exist and their likelihood. It is designed to show you *what can be done* to provide protection and profit.

But no one can tell you *how safe* you want to be. No one can tell you whether or not it is a rational decision to stay off freeways because of the danger created by speeding cars. No one can tell you how much medical insurance is necessary—because no one can determine for you the risks you are willing to take on your own. And no one can tell you how much you're willing to gamble in order to make a fortune.

Once aware of what can happen, *you* will have to decide what to do about it. The investment program outlined in the last chapter tends toward the safe side. You can take greater risks if you like. But even within that program there is a wide latitude of choices for you to make.

This chapter will acquaint you with some of those choices. It will also provide some alternatives. And we will set up a basic table—showing the distribution of your assets among the six investments.

In fact, a seventh category will be included: "other investments." That category is an amount you can use to continue investing in stocks or other speculative areas. Thus you will not have to feel that you have dropped out of civilization entirely.

Please bear in mind that all figures presented are *guides* to help you make decisions for yourself. After you've set up your own investment program, reappraise it once again—asking yourself if the decisions you're making are really in tune with your own nature and your own way of doing things.

Now, a closer look at each of the recommended investments.

CASH

There is very little to say regarding the amount of cash you need or how to get it. Obviously, you obtain it at any commercial bank.

The important thing is to have the cash somewhere, outside of a bank, where you know it will be available to you in case the banks close. If that happens, the general demand for cash may be so great that you can make unusually profitable purchases with your cash.

In some cities, there are companies (not banks) that offer safe-deposit boxes. If you can't find such an alternative, consider building a safe into your home. It may be possible to insure a certain amount of cash against theft.

SWISS FRANCS

The Swiss franc account is for your savings. It will provide the liquidity and safety you need in the event of a depression. It will also be a useful hedge against devaluation.

Many people would consider it overly cautious to put one's savings in a bank thousands of miles away. And yet, in 1933, there must have been millions of Americans who would have been better off had their savings been far away from the bank on the corner when it closed.

In addition, there are multitudes of Europeans who will testify to the wisdom of keeping funds in Switzerland. We are just beginning to see in America the things that they take for granted over there: restrictions on currency exchange, price controls, privacy invasions, etc. In another few years, the value of having funds in Switzerland may be obvious; but it may be too late to do anything about it.

Any fairly large American bank will probably have the American Banking Association's international directory of banks. From this, you can pick the names of three or four Swiss banks. Write to them for the particulars of opening a *Swiss franc deposit account.*

You may find your correspondent's English to be of a slightly different style from your own; but a savings account does not pose too many complications.

Contrary to popular opinion, you do not *pay* to have your funds in such a deposit account. There *are* some accounts for which you pay a fee; but you don't need that kind of account.

A deposit account will pay in the neighborhood of four to five percent interest. There are withdrawal restrictions, but the banks do not enforce them. Instead, you may forfeit a year's interest or six months' interest by a premature withdrawal. Ask the bank to explain this when you write your first letter.

When you open the account, you can send the funds by purchasing a cashier's check at any commercial bank. Air mail postage to Switzerland (in 1970) is 20¢ per half-ounce.

SILVER COINS

The presence of silver coins in the program is *not* intended as a typical capital-appreciation investment. It is to provide real spending money if a runaway inflation should come. The coins *will* appreciate in value, as the price of silver goes up, but that isn't the object.

The coins form a small percentage of your overall program. Their purpose is liquidity in time of crisis.

In 1965, the government converted to the new coinage system. Prior to that time, all dimes, quarters and half-dollars were 90% silver (this includes all coins dated 1964 or earlier). Since the change, the dimes and quarters have *no* silver in them; and the silver content of the halves has been reduced to 40%. *No coin dated 1965 or later should be included in your reserve.*

The silver dollars have achieved a numismatic (coin-collecting) value that makes them too expensive for the purposes with which we are concerned.

Half-dollars, because of their greater scarcity, are commanding a higher premium in the market. But the dimes and quarters are actually better suited for our purposes. The smaller denominations provide greater divisibility; you may not be able to get change for a silver half-dollar in the aftermath of a runaway inflation.

Most coin dealers have silver coins available for sale. They charge a premium over the face value of the coins. For example, if the price quoted is a 15% premium, that means 1,000 dimes ($100 face value) will sell for $115. During 1968 and 1969, premiums ranged from 10% to 40%.

Now that it is legal to melt silver coins, coin prices will be tied more closely to bullion prices. Since the prices are expressed in two different ways, it is necessary to make a translation. To see how this works, let us take a bag of dimes, quarters, or halves amounting to $1,000 face value. If the coins have not been in circulation, there will be 725 troy ounces of silver in the bag. More likely, the coins *will* have circulated, and some of the silver will have been eroded through wear. Such bags average 719 ounces of silver.

To purchase the bag at face value means you're paying $1,000 for 719 ounces of silver. That's $1.39 for each ounce ($1,000 divided by 719). Thus circulated dimes, halves, and quarters have a silver content equal to $1.39 per ounce when the coins are purchased at face value.

At this stage, however, the coins are not comparable to silver bullion. They must be melted and refined to what is called ".999 fine" quality. That cost will vary from smelter to smelter and also depends on the quantity involved. But seven cents per ounce is a realistic average.

If the current price of silver bullion were $1.46 per ounce, silver coins would be selling at about their face value, with no premium. For the $1.39 per ounce content added to the seven cents per ounce charge for melting and refining totals $1.46 to produce one ounce of bullion.

We can create a formula, then, to determine the approximate premium that will be charged on silver coins in order to make them comparable to current bullion prices. The formula is:

(*Current bullion price* — 7¢) × .719 = *silver value per $1 of coins*.

Take the current silver bullion price, subtract 7 cents, and multiply by .719. That will give you the silver value per dollar of face value.[1]

For example, suppose the current bullion price is $2.00 per ounce. In that case, the formula works as follows: ($2.00 — .07) × .719 = $1.38767. Rounded off, that's $1.39 silver value in coins of one dollar face value. The premium, based upon bullion value, is 39% over face value.

1. If the coins are uncirculated, use .725 instead of .719.

But there's a greater value to the silver coins *just because they are coins* (just as a gold necklace is worth more than its gold content). As a result, we can expect the coins to continue selling at a price higher than their silver bullion value. That extra premium will fluctuate; but I expect it to remain around 10% until runaway inflation seems imminent (at which time it should go up drastically). So at a $2.00 bullion price, coins should be selling at a total premium of about 49%.

This additional premium makes it unprofitable for coins to be melted. It would be a case of paying to transform something of one value into something of less value. Consequently, the silver coins will never solve the silver shortage.

The following table shows the probable silver coin premium (above face value) you'll have to pay at any given current silver bullion price. The premiums have been computed from the formula with an extra 10% added for the reasons given above.

CONVERSION OF BULLION PRICES TO SILVER COIN PREMIUMS

Current Bullion Price	Premium on Silver Coins
$1.60	20%
1.70	27%
1.80	34%
1.90	42%
2.00	49%
2.10	56%
2.20	63%
2.30	70%
2.40	78%
2.50	85%
2.60	92%
2.70	99%
2.80	106%
2.90	113%
3.00	121%

If you cannot find a local source for coins, contact the Pacific Coast Coin Exchange, 3520 Long Beach Blvd., Long Beach, California 90807. The owners specialize in silver coins; and they are well acquainted with the silver market and the inflationary problems of today. They ship coins nationwide and even overseas. The cost of shipping from coast to coast adds about 2% more to the premium.

Wherever you buy, make sure that you are getting, and paying for, what it is you really want. Coin dealers are operating in three different markets:

1. The *numismatic market* is for rare coins—of special dates, special mintings, etc. These coins command high premiums above their face value and are of no special use for silver purposes or as protection against runaway inflation. You will pay unnecessarily high prices for rare coins.[2]

2. The *silver commodity market* is the potential of the silver coins to supplement the supply of silver bullion. Since the coins will appreciate as the price of bullion appreciates, you can purchase coins instead of bullion for the bullion part of your budget. As long as you're willing to risk keeping the coins in an American bank, you can finance the face value of the coins and pay only the premium in cash. The Pacific Coast Coin Exchange is the main American source for this type of transaction.

3. *Junk silver* is the label attached to silver coins that have been retrieved from circulation and have no special numismatic value. They normally come in bags, of coins amounting to $1,000 in face value. These coins are the sure source of purchasing power, good in any future conditions. And this *is* what you are looking for.

If you intend to hold a large amount of silver coins, you may want to use any funds in excess of $1,000 to purchase *gold* coins instead. The greater value of gold makes them easier to store.

With plenty of silver coins, you will have the immediate day-to-day spending money you may need. The gold coins can be used to purchase larger items—land, facilities, etc.—or they can be traded for a supply of silver coins.

2. The investment potential of this market is discussed on page 117.

The best coins for this purpose would be American $20 gold pieces.

SILVER BULLION

When silver finally rose in 1967, from its pegged price of $1.29 per ounce, it became an object of widespread speculation. Many individuals who did not invest wisely lost money when the price slid from its mid-1968 high of $2.55 per ounce. They had purchased on too risky a margin basis and could not cover their margin calls when the price dropped all the way to $1.55.

This points up an important consideration: *when investing, always determine first the objective of your investment.* Many of the individuals who lost money in the silver slides suffered from a factor that should not have affected them. They were concerned about depreciating currency; and their objective was to find a stable value that would protect their savings.

Silver was an ideal investment, even at $2.50 per ounce. For the drop was inevitably temporary. And over the long term, their savings would regain their value and appreciate.

The problem arose when these people bought on margin, merely because other people were buying that way. They purchased silver with equities as low as 25% or 20%. It does not take a very big price drop to wipe out such a thin equity.

If these people had purchased on a cash basis, the price drop would not have affected them permanently. Instead, they lost all they had.

The incentive to buy on margin was, of course, the hope of a much greater gain. This is quite all right—in the right circumstances.

But a simple question was overlooked. One should always ask oneself: which of the two risks can I *least* afford—(1) the possibility that I will not make as much profit if the price goes up? or (2) the possibility that I could lose my entire investment if the price goes down?

For some, it is a go-for-broke investment. The loss of one's capital is a calculated risk against the hope of making one's whole fortune on this one investment. But for many, losing the investment meant the destruction of 30 years' savings.

It is important, therefore, to make your own decisions as to the purpose of the investment, what you can afford to risk, and how you will approach it.

For reasons we have already discussed, it is best to buy and store the bullion outside the country. The most practical and obvious way of doing this is through a Swiss bank.

Although it is not very difficult to open a savings account in a Swiss bank, it is a good deal harder to find one that will buy silver bullion for you—especially if you wish to use margin.

Many of the banks prefer to buy "forward contracts" for you. These require no bank financing and a minimum of effort by the bank. This is *not* what you want, however. Forward contracts are for a specified period of time, with prepaid interest. They are not as flexible as contracts to buy bullion, with the bank financing part of the purchase.

Economic Research Counselors (P.O. Box 368, San Diego, California 92112) is one firm that has specialized in arranging silver bullion purchases through Swiss banks since 1966. If you contact them, they can acquaint you with their program and put you in touch with banks that will handle the kind of purchases we're reviewing here. Since it is not always easy to communicate with Swiss bankers, it is often advisable to use an intermediary.

There is nothing wrong with margin buying if you are primarily interested in capital appreciation, are aware of the risks, and are willing to take them. The process is referred to as *leverage*— meaning the use of someone else's money to enlarge your participation in the market.

For example, three-to-one leverage works as follows: For every dollar you send to the bank, it lends you two dollars—making a total of three dollars. You then purchase three dollars worth of silver with a one-dollar investment (three to one).

You pay interest on the borrowed money. The interest rate may fluctuate during the time you hold the silver, since you have no specific termination date for the loan; it will be repaid when you finally sell the silver.

If the price drops substantially from your purchase price, you will get a *margin call*. The lower price for silver will mean that the value of your holdings is dropping close to the amount you owe the bank. So a margin call is a request that you pay off part of the loan. This creates a wider margin between the amount of the loan and the current value of the silver.

If you buy on two-to-one leverage, at $2.00 per ounce or less, the chances of getting a margin call are no more than one in a hundred. But, on any other basis, you should be prepared for the possibility of a margin call.

Policies vary from bank to bank, and even from time to time within the same bank, but the following table will give you a rough idea of what to expect.

CAUSES AND AMOUNTS OF MARGIN CALLS

Leverage used:	1–1	2–1	3–1	4–1
Drop from purchase price to cause a margin call:[3]	—	35%	15%	5%
Amount of margin call as % of original investment:	—	7%	15%	20%

Here's an example: Suppose you invest $1,000 at three-to-one leverage and purchase at $2.00 per ounce. Referring to the table above, we see that it would require a price drop of 15% to cause a margin call; and that the margin call would be approximately the equivalent of 15% of your original investment. That means you could expect a margin call at $2.00 less 15% or $1.70. And your margin call would probably be about 15% of your original investment, meaning you would be asked to pay about $150 against your loan.

3. Assumes a period of six months after purchase, with interest, brokerage, and storage charges added to loan whenever due.

If you buy at three-to-one or four-to-one leverage, you should have the required margin payment available, even if you never need it. The best way to handle it is to have your Swiss franc savings account in the same bank. Tell the bank to draw upon the savings account for margin payments, if ever needed. That way you never need fear that you won't receive the margin call or that it will arrive too late.

Your attitude toward such an investment can be classified perhaps under one of the following four headings:

Safety only: You desire only to preserve the capital you have; and are not interested in taking any risks, even to make a large profit.

Conservative: You are looking for a good profit; but you fear loss of your capital much more than loss of added profits. You are prepared for the possibility of a margin call.

Normally speculative: You are willing to take risks, will meet a margin call if necessary, and are hoping to make an excellent profit from the investment.

Quite speculative: The original investment is not precious to you. You are quite willing to risk it against the possibility of making an unusually large profit. You are prepared to meet a margin call.

AMOUNT OF LEVERAGE APPROPRIATE
(Based upon price range and attitude of purchaser)

Price Range	Quite Speculative	Normally Speculative	Conservative	Safety Only
$1.80 or less	4–1	3–1	3–1	2–1
$1.81–2.00	4–1	3–1	2½–1	1–1 or 2–1
$2.01–2.25	3–1	2½–1	2½–1	1–1
$2.26–2.50	3–1	2½–1	2–1	1–1
$2.51–3.00	2½–1	2¼–1	2–1	1–1
$3.01–4.00	2½–1	2–1	1–1	1–1
Over $4.00	2–1	1½–1	1–1	1–1

The amount of leverage you use will depend upon which classification fits you, and upon the price range of silver at the time you buy. The preceding table is constructed from those two factors.

For example, if you fit the "normally speculative" classification, and the current price of silver is $2.38 per ounce, the table indicates that leverage of two and one-half to one is appropriate.

This is only a rough guide, however. There are other factors that can enter into the decision. If the price has just jumped 50 cents because of worldwide monetary fears, it may fall right back again, before continuing upward. In such a case, you should use *less* leverage than the table indicates. Professional advice will be helpful.

You will read a great deal about silver in the newspapers, investment advisory services, and news magazines. A great many of the reports are based upon statements emanating originally from the U.S. Treasury. Other surveys can be very superficial and contradictory.

Don't be discouraged by adverse silver news—anymore than you would be swayed by someone's statement that gold is no longer necessary for our monetary systems.

GOLD STOCKS

In a previous chapter, it was recommended that you split your gold stocks between American and South African companies. The devaluation of the dollar is almost inevitable; but this is not the case with the *rand*, the South African currency unit.

American stocks are almost sure to go way up in price within the next two years. Since the rise will be sudden and steep, it is much better to buy too early, rather than to wait for something to happen.

As we have seen, emotional reactions will probably send the South African stocks up, even if only the dollar has been devalued. In addition, South African stocks are generally better bargains than the American group. American gold stocks are in much the same position as other American stocks—they're generally over-priced because of inflation.

Locate a stock broker who is sympathetic to what you are trying to do. Find one who has specialized in gold stocks and make sure his reasons are much the same as yours. You can deal with him, even if he has different ideas about economic conditions. Just be sure you don't leave your fate completely in his hands.

His insight and advice will help you to select the specific stocks to buy. But there are some basic considerations that you can apply to any gold stock.

Most important, pick stocks whose price-to-earnings ratios are not oversized. Some American stocks are selling at fifty times their annual earnings. Those stock prices have no room to grow.

South African stocks, on the whole, have low price-to-earnings ratios. In addition, they are paying high dividends already. You can draw income from them, even while waiting for the spectacular price increases. There are South African stocks that return 6% to 10% in dividends, even after subtracting the 15% interest equalization tax that applies to all foreign stocks.

In addition, there are some companies that are operating in a very marginal position at present gold prices. Those that are just barely breaking even will probably increase more than those that are already showing a good profit.

Some companies are stockpiling their gold at present prices. They sell just enough to pay their bills; the rest is being stored, awaiting higher prices.[4]

As we have already seen, it is safest to sell any gold stock after it drops 5% from its post-devaluation high. South African stocks will probably be appreciating for unrealistic reasons. And American stocks are vulnerable to governmental intervention, once the gold business gets to be too lucrative. So it can be dangerous to hold any gold stock too long.

It is possible to purchase stocks through the Swiss bank that

4. I am grateful to John H. Weber, a broker with Rutner, Jackson & Gray in Los Angeles, for calling some of these matters to my attention.

handles your savings account and silver bullion purchases. The principal argument against doing so is the need for precise timing in liquidating the stocks after the devaluation. Raise the question with the Swiss banker and see what he suggests.

If you are *not* an American citizen, consider using part of your gold budget for gold bullion—for further diversification. That can be handled through the Swiss bank.

THE RETREAT

The retreat budget is really a *safety* budget. It is the creation of whatever protection you feel you need, to avoid being caught up in the chaos that may take place if runaway inflation strikes.

For one person it may be a well-stocked camper and a roadmap. For another, an elaborate hideaway—complete with every comfort that can be afforded. For still another, it may be plans to move to a foreign city. Or it may just be more elaborate protection where you live right now.

Whatever it is, it must be something *you* can live with. It must provide the degree of protection you demand; and it must also be a kind of life that you can tolerate. Don't plan unrealistically to live in a way that you've never even experienced.

What you do will depend a great deal on where you live now. What would the environment be like if the currency became worthless? Would your present neighborhood be safe?

Try to make whatever you create serve a dual purpose. Make it usable for vacations, so that you will not be investing everything in disaster insurance.

Once you attempt the job of setting up a realistic retreat, you begin to discover an endless list of questions that must be answered. There are considerations of electricity, water, waste disposal, protection, etc.

There is a great body of literature available to answer the various questions that will occur to you. And there are many products already on the market that will serve useful purposes. But it requires a lot of digging to find it all.

As far as I know, there's only one book on the market that lists source material that has been compiled specifically for these purposes. That is *The Retreater's Bibliography*, listed in the bibliography in the back of this book.

INVEST IN YOURSELF

There is one more investment that should not be overlooked. Invest in *enjoyment*. There may be many tasty things you have been looking forward to. You may have planned to indulge yourself with these things in later years.

Those things may not be available, however, if the worst does happen. You will have worked and saved for opportunities that may not exist when the time comes.

Enjoy yourself now. You can't avoid the responsibility you have to protect your future and your family's future. But, at the same time, don't pass up the opportunity to enjoy the tasty things of life, while you still can.

Pick the rewards that are meaningful to you and taste some of them now, whether they be grand opera, expensive cars, traveling, or good clothes. What is a luxury to you today may not be available at all if runaway inflation should come.

HOW MUCH FOR EACH INVESTMENT?

At the outset of this chapter, I pointed out that only you can determine how safe you want to be. You will have to decide for yourself how to distribute your present assets in accordance with your own values.

The table on page 169 may be helpful to you as a *guide* in arranging that distribution. It shows a division of your funds, based upon the total amount of assets. An individual with a larger estate will have a different arrangement than one with a smaller estate will have.

In the smaller estate, there will be a larger percentage in cash, silver coins, and the retreat. In the higher brackets, the emphasis will be more on gold stocks and other investments. Silver bullion receives greater attention in the medium brackets, while Swiss francs receive less in the middle brackets.

In the higher brackets, there is a budget for "other investments." This assumes that, after providing basic protection, you may still want to speculate in other investments—hoping your timing will be precise enough to reap the best of both worlds. That may include supplementary recommendations from this book, such as short selling. Or it may mean staying in the stock market until the last possible moment. In any case, allowance is made for such investments in the higher brackets of the table. Again, this is only a guide.

THE INVESTMENT PROGRAM — BASED UPON AMOUNT OF ASSETS

Amount of Money to be Used

Item	$5,000	$10,000	$20,000	$50,000	$100,000	$1,000,000
Cash in dollars	$ 750	$ 750	$ 1,000	$ 2,500	$ 5,000	$ 50,000
Swiss francs	1,000	1,750	3,500	7,500	15,000	200,000
Silver coins	250	500	1,000	1,000	2,000*	20,000*
Silver bullion	1,500	4,000	7,500	17,500	35,000	250,000
Gold stocks	500	1,000	2,500	10,000	20,000	200,000
Retreat	1,000	2,000	2,500	5,000	10,000	80,000
Other investments	—	—	2,000	6,500	13,000	200,000

*Includes gold coins.

$ CHAPTER 20 $

The New Millionaires

$ $ $ $ $

NOW IT IS UP TO YOU. I HAVE PASSED ON TO YOU THE INSIGHT AND information that I have. But positive action can come only from you. You must see a need to take steps to separate yourself from the prevailing clichés and false confidence.

If you do, it may prove to be one of the most important decisions you've ever made in your life. Not only will it free you from the vulnerabilities facing millions of others; but it will provide the foundation and opportunity upon which you can build a new, larger fortune for yourself.

You will hear—right up to the crisis—all the typical platitudes, asserting that the dollar is absolutely sound, that "we have nothing to fear but fear itself," that "depressions are caused by fear mongers," etc. But we have seen the fundamental economic principles that transcend confidence and mass psychology. We have seen that certain things are inevitable, even if *everyone* is convinced they can't happen.

This brings us right back to where we started in the first chapter. Certain things *are* going to happen. You can see them coming. You'll either profit from them or be hurt by them. Which of the two applies will depend wholly upon you. What will you do?

The choice is yours—to go along with the tide or take steps to avoid the tide of history in your own life. No matter what may happen to others, it doesn't have to happen to you. But only you can make that choice.

If you decide to do something about this, the time to do it is right now. If you want to play the game of waiting until the last moment, realize the stakes involved. You're playing with your own future, as well as the future of your family.

You can take some short-term flyers, if that suits your temperament and ambition. But get your house in order first; then use the funds you can afford to risk and have a ball.

But, above all, recognize the consequences. Don't keep playing in the stock market if you can't afford the consequences of getting out too late. Don't be like the man with six kids who bets his paycheck at the racetrack. And remember, too, that gamblers never know when to quit.

Even after deciding to act upon the suggestions of this book, you will have further choices to make. As I've mentioned several times, the recommendations can only be a guide. You will have to make the ultimate decisions for yourself.

There is nothing rigid about the investment program suggested. You certainly don't have to do what I do—or vice versa. It depends upon *your* sense of values—what you want—what you can afford and can't afford—what you are willing to risk and what you can't risk.

I happen to be single, in the prime of my big earning years. I can afford to risk capital that maybe you can't risk. I feel I can always earn back what I lose; and if I'm right, I intend to make it all at once.

So, within the framework of the considerations of this book, I am willing to be quite speculative. But that would be totally inappropriate for a widow on a pension.

Do what will allow you to sleep nights during the period of uncertainty that is ahead.

TIMING

It is very difficult to establish the timing of coming events. You can only take the attitude that it will be better to have been two years too early, rather than a day too late.

I have tried testing various signals to see if timing can be gauged. I've decided it isn't worth the trouble. There are so many contradictory signals and causes that you cannot possibly be aware of all of them.

As the year 1969 opened, Federal Reserve official George Mitchell stated that the Federal Reserve System was working to maintain a constant money supply. That would imply a slowdown in the rate of inflation, wouldn't it?

During the second week of January, the paper money supply *increased by two billion dollars*. If that pattern were kept up for a year, it would mean an annual rate of increase of 50%![1]

Don't pay any attention to statements of intention or opinions or plans or hopes or anything from government officials. They are totally meaningless as guides to coming action.

At any given time, you are most likely to see inflationary elements on one side, accompanied by deflationary factors on the other. You just can't know for sure which inputs will prevail.

There is one thing that is certain. Big changes are coming and they are not very far away. There is no way to avoid them. Neither is there any way you can control them. But you can make sure not only that they don't destroy you, but that you will profit from them.

In the spring of 1966, I told an economics class that I felt the crisis would hit us during a period between one and five years from then. That would place the outer limits at the spring of 1971. I have seen no reason to change my mind in the interim.

If I'm wrong and we have more time than that left, wonderful! I can use all the time there is. I love opera and concerts and many of the things our present environment offers. They may be

1. Reported in *Indicator Digest*, January 21, 1969.

in very short supply once the crisis hits. So I'll be grateful for every month they're with us.

But I'm not going to count on any extra time. It is important instead that my house be in order and that I then live every day, one at a time, enjoying what life has to offer, and ready to take advantage of the new circumstances to come.

If the future outlined in this book *never* comes, I will not have lost. If I have somehow made a gross error in my calculations (very, very unlikely), I will not have thrown away my life on the projection. For the investment program will profit from a continuation of the *status quo*. And I'm sure I can somehow adapt to conditions of general prosperity.

As you discuss this with others, you may hear an argument that goes something like this: "Of course, no rational person can overlook the possibility that we might have another depression in this country. But that is no reason to sacrifice everything for that one eventuality. If a depression *should* come, we will get plenty of warning in advance. There are *signals* that can warn you to get out before it's too late."

Those *signals* are going to cause one of the greatest panics in the history of the American financial market. The pseudo-sophistication enjoyed by the stock broker is shared by every reader of a financial advisory service, every client of a stock broker or investment adviser, every reader of the financial pages of the local newspaper.

It is the very existence of those *signals* that moves the market with such great force in one direction or another today. Those *signals* are shared by millions of people. And when their message is "depression coming!" they will cause a mass sell-off of stocks that will drive the market down by hundreds of points—without a single buyer to cover anyone's intended sale.

Certainly, the signals may tell you when to get out. *But you can't get out if there's no one willing to buy your stock.*

Reread Chapter Nine. Remind yourself that in the twenties there were plenty of people who knew the signals. And on October

29, 1929, they saw the signals clearly and tried to sell. But everyone else saw the signals, too; and there were no buyers.

To get out too early means that you must have patience. You must be willing to sit on the sidelines, watch others scoop up a few more dollars and call to you, "See, it hasn't hurt yet!"

You will find yourself in the position of a man whose next-door neighbor doesn't believe in insurance. You watch that neighbor indulge himself in all sorts of extra luxuries that you cannot afford.

Those luxuries are paid for, however, with money that should have gone into insurance premiums—for fire insurance on the house, car insurance, medical insurance. Will the neighbor be right if he says, "See, I haven't had a fire or an accident or an illness, why do I need insurance?"

You answer him. Is he right or is he wrong? If he's right, disregard the lessons of this book. If he's wrong, don't worry about his taunts and smugness and temporary profits; do what *you* have to do to get *your* house in order.

YOUR FUTURE

If your reaction to this book is a slightly depressed mood, I can't blame you. And yet, at the same time, there really is no reason for such a reaction.

This book was not written to shock you, to take away some happiness and contentment from your life, nor to be merely the bearer of bad news. If it has seemed only a Cassandra wail, then I haven't made myself very clear.

In the first place, haven't you already been a bit uneasy about this whole subject? You didn't pick up this book with the attitude that the economic future was blissful, did you?

This book has permitted you to face up to your uneasiness once and for all—so that you can finally do something about it. Up to now, the subject has been a source of discomfort to you. Now you can get your house in order and relax for a change.

Now you can set things right in your life and get on with the business of living. Your conscience will be clear and your mind will be free. Then you can enjoy life in earnest, knowing that you have done all you could to eliminate the dark vulnerabilities from your life.

Life is easy and wonderful when you know you're not living in Fantasyland, when you know you've faced reality and are dealing with it.

Ignorance is *not* bliss. It is a source of destruction.

Reality is bliss, once it has been faced and dealt with.

But there is far more than just security and protection involved here. After every crisis, new millionaires are created. It is not that they profit from misery; it is that they are the individuals of foresight. They are the true benefactors of society, the ones who have conserved some wealth and kept it from the destructive hands of the bureaucrats. They have it available to build a new society from the ashes of the old one, the society that was destroyed by the insatiable appetites of governments.

That is the economic future—a future in which there will be new financial empires, new luxuries, a new life for everyone. Whether your new life will be better or worse than the old one will depend upon what you do now.

Your ability to act now with foresight will make it possible for you to be ready for what is coming. But you must recognize that your responsibility is to yourself and not to the government. No one can possibly live the life of someone else—and yet, you will be asked to do so.

Your patriotism will be appealed to: "Buy bonds"—"save the banks"—"don't rock the boat"—"don't undermine confidence"— "invest in America." But react by saving *yourself*, not the government.

Be careful how the word "we" is thrown around. People often say to me, "Isn't it terrible what we've done to the value of the dollar?" I always feel like replying, "I didn't know *you* were a party to the crime. But please don't include me in that 'we'— I didn't have anything to do with it."

You are not responsible for what has happened; it is the government that has destroyed the currency. Even if you have had your own hand in the trough in the past, don't allow yourself to be overcome by guilt. You didn't create the system.

Once having recognized the system, you'll do a lot for your self-esteem if you get *off* the gravy train and make an honest living. But don't allow your past acts to engulf you in a sense of responsibility for what is happening.

The mistakes have been made by power-hungry individuals who wanted to play God with the lives and resources of the American people. Their schemes are coming to an inevitably tragic end.

And as that end nears, they will appeal to that "we" for help. They will appeal to unity, to patriotism, to anything they can—hoping that *you'll* pay the price of their mistakes.

Don't do it.

You have no legal or moral commitment to throw *your* wealth into the fire along with all the rest that is being destroyed.

If you're determined to be altruistic about it, the only way you can be of any good to anyone is to be self-sufficient. The biggest burdens in a crisis are those who were so concerned about the welfare of everyone else that they never provided for themselves. That doesn't seem particularly noble, does it?

So much of the world's precious resources are wasted by individuals who think they can save the world—when they haven't even made provisions for saving themselves.

You have only one mission: *to survive and prosper*. That should be all-important for the next few months until you get your house in order.

It is not your responsibility to save the world. You are responsible for only one person: *you*.

You can count on only one person to provide the protection you need. And that, too, is *you*

But if you face up to the problem and quit wishing that it would go away—if you eliminate from your mind all the false responsibilities and clichés—you'll find there are new fortunes to be made.

There *will* be new Andrew Carnegies after the next crisis. The degree of profit will depend largely upon the capital one begins with. But anyone who faces up to what is coming can improve his position many times over.

And if *you* face up to what is coming, and *you* do what is necessary to secure your future (not the world's future), and *you* have the patience and foresight to await the inevitable, the rewards will be there.

And guess who will reap those rewards?

That's right: *you!*

Isn't your future worth it?

Glossary

Barter:
: The trading of an individual's property for another commodity he intends to use himself. (Direct exchange.)

Capital goods:
: Products whose only purpose is to produce other products.

Coins:
: Real money transformed into a recognizable shape and weight in order to facilitate exchange.

Currency:
: Money substitutes in paper form.

Deflation:
: A decrease in the amount of money substitutes that are in excess of the stored stock of real money.

Demand deposit:
: The storing of your money in a bank, but still available on demand, for which you usually pay a fee.

Depression:
: The liquidation period following a prolonged inflationary cycle; and/or a liquidation period in which governmental restraint of trade prevents orderly liquidation, thereby prolonging a recession.

Devaluation:
: Repudiation of the government's promise to honor its money substitutes at the stated rate of exchange.

Direct exchange:
: The trading of an individual's property for another commodity he intends to use himself. (Barter.)

General price level:
: The available money supply divided by the goods and services available for sale.

Indirect exchange:	The trading of an individual's property for another commodity he does not intend to use himself.
Inflation:	An increase in money substitutes above the stored stock of real money.
Liquidation:	Normally, the sale of a property. With regard to recessions and depressions, *liquidation* refers to the acceptance of losses and the closing of businesses that existed only because of the miscalculations caused by inflation.
Money:	A commodity that is accepted in exchange by an individual who intends to trade it for something else.
Money receipt:	A receipt that can be readily exchanged for real money.
Money substitutes:	Money receipts and demand deposits that are used in exchange, in place of real money.
Paper money:	Receipts for real money in storage.
Paper money supply:	Currency outside of banks, plus checking account deposits, plus tokens.
Real money:	Gold or silver—in bullion, dust, or coinage.
Recession:	The liquidation period following an inflationary period.
Runaway inflation:	An inflationary period in which the paper money supply increases fast enough to cause prices to change at least daily.

Time Deposit: The lending of your money to a bank,
                           not to be available for a specified period
                           of time, for which you receive a fee
                           (interest).

Token: A money substitute in metallic form,
                           rather than paper.

Bibliography

Bibliographies are notorious as sources of misinformation. An author carefully lists every piece of literature that has contributed any information to his work. The reader, with no roadmap to guide him, makes the mistake of securing some of the books listed—only to find them of no practical value to his own objectives.

Listed below are 18 books or booklets that contain valuable information on one or more of the facets of this book. A short description is given to prepare you for what you will find in the book.

MONEY

1. Bakewell, Paul: *Thirteen Curious Errors About Money.* A sound and easy-to-follow discussion of some of the common monetary fallacies and how they have been applied to the dollar in the past 40 years. It also contains the full text of the U.S. Gold Regulations. Published by Caxton Printers, Caldwell, Idaho; $2.00.

2. *Pick's Currency Yearbook.* An expensive, but helpful, annual guide to currencies, exchange rates, inflationary characteristics, gold supplies, exchange restrictions, in all nations of the world. Published by Pick Publishing Company, New York, New York 10006; $70.00 per annual edition.

3. Rickenbacker, William F.: *Death of the Dollar.* An easy-to-read background of the developing crisis. The author lists dozens of symptoms. Published by Arlington House, New Rochelle, New York; $4.95.

4. Rothbard, Murray N.: *What Has Government Done to Our Money?* A 49-page booklet that quickly summarizes the purpose of money and how governments have distorted that purpose. Published by Rampart College, 102 W. Fourth St., Santa Ana, California; $1.00.

5. von Mises, Ludwig: *The Theory of Money and Credit.* This

is a textbook and should not be thought of as "light reading." It is the basic statement on money by what is called the "Austrian school of economics." Published by Yale University Press, New Haven, Connecticut; $7.00.

THE FEDERAL RESERVE SYSTEM

6. *The Federal Reserve System, Purposes and Functions.* This "official" book is helpful for specific information regarding the mechanics of the system. It even explains how money is created. The Federal Reserve System also publishes a series of periodicals providing information on changes in the money supply and other national economic data. Ask for a list of the publications. Published by the Board of Governors, Federal Reserve System, Washington, D.C.; no charge for the book.

INFLATION

7. Hazlitt, Henry: *What You Should Know About Inflation.* Henry Hazlitt is a master of clarity, and this short book provides a general picture of inflation, how it is created, and where it leads. Published by Van Nostrand, Princeton, New Jersey; $3.50.

8. White, Andrew Dickson: *Fiat Money Inflation in France.* A potent antidote to those who believe that "a little inflation" is good for the economy. This is a case history of the destruction of the French currency during the Revolution. Published by Caxton Printers, Caldwell, Idaho; $1.00.

DEPRESSIONS

9. Patterson, Robert T.: *The Great Boom and Panic.* A well-written chronicle of the stock market in 1929. No attempt is made to explain the cause of the depression; but it provides helpful insights into the nature of confidence-building and bubble-bursting. Published by Henry Regnery Company, Chicago, Illinois 60610; $6.50.

10. Rothbard, Murray N.: *America's Great Depression.* Painstakingly prepared, this book is the story of America from 1921 to

1933. It details the inflation of the twenties and the depression of the early thirties. It lays to rest dozens of historical fallacies, and establishes beyond doubt the government's responsibility for the crisis. It is not easy reading, however; it is a textbook, heavily documented, and meticulously precise. Published by Van Nostrand, Princeton, New Jersey; $8.95.

11. Rothbard, Murray N.: *The Panic of* 1819. This book is easier to read than *America's Great Depression* and its theoretical sections are simpler. A very clear explanation of the inflation-depression cycle is given. In terms of historical information, however, it is further removed from us. It also demonstrates the degree of governmental intervention as far back as 1819. Published by Columbia University Press, New York City, New York 10027; $6.00.

ECONOMICS IN GENERAL

12. Hazlitt, Henry: *Economics in One Lesson.* There are a number of sound books for the student of economics (although they are not widely used in university economics courses today). I will not attempt to lay out a reading list for the individual who wants to pursue the subject in earnest. Instead, this little book is included because its purpose is to alert the mind to ward off clichés and typical economic fallacies. Published in paperback by Macfadden Publications, New York City, New York 10017; 50 cents.

SILVER

13. Butts, Allison and Coxe, Charles D.: *Silver—Economics, Metallurgy, and Use.* A scholarly work delving into the geology, recovery, production, and industrial consumption of silver. Recommended only for those who want a thorough knowledge of the subject. Published by Van Nostrand, Princeton, New Jersey; $15.00.

14. Rickenbacker, William F.: *Wooden Nickels.* This, too, contains a good deal of the background on the availability of silver and the demand for it. However, this book was written to provide back-

ground for the end of silver coinage; so it is not as geared to silver as an investment as is *The Economics of Silver*, below. It is an interesting commentary on how inflation drove precious metals out of the coins. Published by Arlington House, New Rochelle, New York; $3.95.

15. Smith, Jerome F.: *The Economics of Silver*. This short booklet provides all of the essential statistics and information concerning the silver market. I am grateful to the author, Jerome F. Smith, for some of the material on silver included in this book. Published by Economic Research Counselors, Box 368, San Diego, California 92112; $5.00.

GOLD AS AN INVESTMENT

16. Gilbert, Robert A.: *Gold Mining Shares*. Written in late 1967, this is a brief study of gold mining stocks in the United States, Canada, and South Africa. Published by Investors' Press, Palisades Park, New Jersey.

SWISS BANKS

17. Fehrenbach T. R.: *The Swiss Banks*. The history and mechanics of the Swiss banks; very engrossing reading. There is a good deal of practical information regarding the banks, interspersed among a number of interesting stories. Published by McGraw-Hill Company, New York, New York 10036; $6.95.

RETREATS

18. Stephens, Don and Barbara: *The Retreater's Bibliography*. An indispensable booklet of supply sources and literature available for the individual interested in establishing a retreat. Available from Don Stephens, 5020 Elverano Avenue, Los Angeles, California 90041; $9.50.

Index

DATE DUE

FEB 1 1 2000

GAYLORD   #3523PI   Printed in USA

Clackamas Community College Library